I like to believe that I was born near Sedona because I am meant to work with the vortices. Those who take the time to read this book will find that I have a native understanding of the subject that sets me apart from other teachers.

At the time of this writing, this is the most in-depth and detailed book on this subject. I do not, however, claim to know all there is to know about the vortices or Earth Energy. It is important to understand that all of us are taking part in this great adventure together. I am merely the one that the earth has chosen to gather this information.

Interest in the vortex phenomenon is not a passing fad. It is instead one of the signs that the human race is developing planetary consciousness and rediscovering its spiritual nature. We are the children of the earth, and we have traditionally sought inspiration and healing in places where the spirit of the earth is strong. It is natural for us to seek out power spots: as modern Americans we are merely rediscovering the ancient ways.

The call of the earth has long been ignored, but within our hearts it has never been forgotten. People are drawn to Sedona because they instinctively know that they need the earth's boost to reawaken their mystical connection with the earth, and the universe itself.

Vortices can supply such a boost. Simply stated, a vortex is a place where the energy of the earth is particularly strong. By learning how to "tune in" to this energy we can increase our natural psychic abilities.

The vortex phenomenon can be understood in scientific, spiritual or metaphysical terms. Scientific types will be happy to know that "Earth Energy" is not an intangible metaphysical substance. Earth Energy is the electromagnetic field of the earth. NASA research has proven that our central nervous systems are "tuned" to an "earth wave" (natural radio wave which is produced by the earth) which oscillates at between 7-8 cycles per second.

The theta brain wave state, which is associated with deep relaxation, meditation and certain forms of paranormal psychic experiences, also occurs between 7-8 cycles per second. This means that when our brain waves are at the same frequency as the earth wave we have tuned in to what could metaphorically be called the "heartbeat of the mother, (by luck or training) enter an altered state of consciousness which may allow us to have the kind of experience that most people just read about.

So much for scientific explanations. There is only so much that can be explained logically. As those who are in a position to know will tell you, there is also spirit. The universe is spirit, our planet is spirit, and all upon it are spirit.

SEDONA POWER SPOT and VORTEX 2000

by
RICHARD DANNELLEY

First Edition

Published by Richard Dannelley
in cooperation with the Sedona Vortex Society
and
SEdONA INformatioN SERViCES

Copyright 2000, Richard Dannelley
ISBN 0-9629453-1-5

Printed in the USA by Light Technology, Sedona, Arizona.

Address all correspondence to:
Richard Dannelley, c/o of the Vortex Society
P.O. Box 948
Sedona, Arizona 86339

vortex@sedona.net
http://www.sedonavortex.org

Book design, hand-drawn graphics, cover and mandala by Richard Dannelley
Meditation graphics Richard Dannelley
Satellite image maps by Richard Dannelley
Planetary grid maps and geometrical figures by David Work
DNA clip art, flying pigs, angels, black helicopters © Corel Corporation
Photography by Richard Dannelley
10 9 8 7 6 5 4 3 2 1

Many people are under the impression that Page Bryant discovered the vortices. She is rightfully credited with being the first to bring forth detailed chan - neled information about these power spots, but she did not discover them.

Modern spiritual seekers have been drawn to Sedona to experience the myster - ies of the Red Rocks since at least as far back as the mid to late fifties. The Chapel of the Holy Cross was built in 1955-56, and the Rainbow Ray Focus was estab - lished near the Airport Vortex in 1963.

The person who should be credited with originally bringing the mysterious power of Sedona into widespread public awareness is Dick Sutphen who, like many others, was drawn here to experience Sedona's energies and grow. Mr. Sutphen has never claimed to have discovered the power spots of Sedona. He freely admits that he learned of the strange power of the place that we now call the Airport Vortex from an acquaintance.

As I cast my memory back in time, I distinctly remember hearing Mr. Sutphen on the Phoenix-area radio station KDKB in 1976 or 1977 speaking about the "mys - terious power spot" near the Sedona airport, and UFO sightings around Bell Rock. This is when I became interested in this subject.

Dick Sutphen published information about the Airport Vortex in 1978 in his book, *Past Lives, Future Loves*. During that period of time he also gave talks at his seminars in the Phoenix area about the mysterious energies of both the Airport Vortex and Bell Rock. In 1980 he spoke on this subject at one of his seminars in Scottsdale, Arizona, at which Page Bryant appeared as a guest speaker.

Mr. Sutphen's lecture seems to be what got Page interested in Sedona, because three months later she came to Sedona and channeled the information about the vortices that inspired so many people. She identified Boynton Canyon and Cathe - dral Rock as major power spots and gave us valuable clues about the nature of the energies we encounter at these places.

Since that time, and during the nine years that the original version of this book has been in print, I have learned quite a bit more about the vortices than was origi - nally given in her channelings.

In Celebration of

Sedona Power Spot and Vortex 2000

I have been exploring the mysteries of the vortex for over 20 years. I am convinced that the energy of Sedona has a magnetic quality that attracts people, and that the energy of these rocks can have a very positive effect on individuals who are open to receive.

The remarkable success the original *Sedona Power Spot, Vortex and Medicine Wheel Guide* enjoyed during the past eight years indicates that our society is rapidly discovering that there is much more to physical existence than meets the eye. I encourage you to join the thousands of people who have already enjoyed this book and experienced the life-changing energies of the universal vortex phenomenon.

This new edition of the *Sedona Power Spot, Vortex and Medicine Wheel Guide* contains important new information and excerpts from my other two books, *Sedona: Beyond the Vortex* and *Sedona UFO Connection*, which has been out of print since 1995. After nine successful years of publication I felt compelled to expand and improve *Sedona Power Spot, Vortex and Medicine Wheel Guide* and realized that I could do my readers a great service by including the segments on meditation, vortex theories and the planetary grid that appear in *Sedona: Beyond the Vortex*. and for fun I also decided to include some material from my book *Sedona UFO Connection, honoring the fact that some of these weird stories deserve telling again.*

The past nine years have been an incredible journey for me and I have spent a significant amount of time and money in the pursuit of knowledge of the secrets of existence, even managing to attend classes given by the mysterious and elusive "Godfather of the New Age," Carlos Castaneda.

I have been able to tap into the powers of the universe and mold my life into something new, and if I can do these things I am sure there are many others who also have this potential. With this new edition I want to reaffirm the truth of what I have learned and pass this on to my readers.

My research has led me to the same conclusion that has been found by philosophers since the most ancient times: **The ultimate secret that will unlock all doors is that the forces of nature are basically quite simple and easy to understand;** *that there is but one energy in the entire universe, and that is love.* If we are able to simplify our thoughts and surrender to the power of love, the forces of nature become our friend and we are accelerated on our journey to back to God.

Richard Dannelley

Table of Contents

MAP SECTION STARTS ON PAGE 26

VISIT PANORAMIC POINT ON PAGE 118

The complex rock formations of Sedona
reveal that this is a particularly active region
in the earth's energy field.

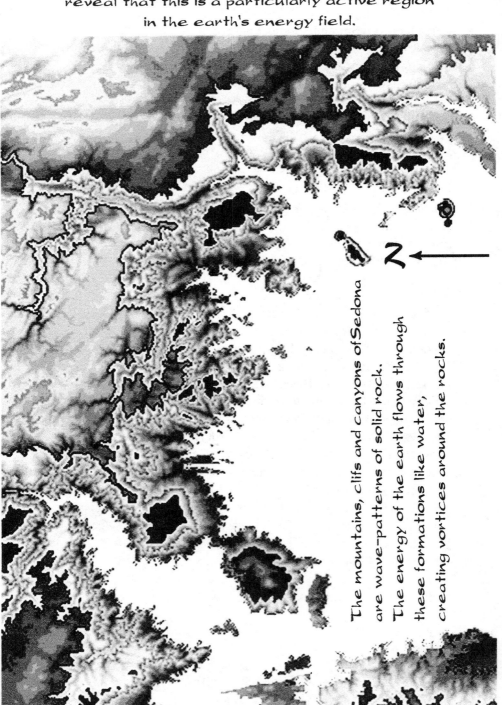

The mountains, clifs and canyons of Sedona
are wave-patterns of solid rock.
The energy of the earth flows through
these formations like water,
creating vortices around the rocks.

Chapter 1

Timeless Wisdom

The Kachina Woman

The Indians who lived in Sedona hundreds of years ago were a mysterious group who may have chosen to live in this difficult and isolated environment because they followed the ancient Toltec Indian spiritual path that teaches that the energy of the earth has the power to help make a person immortal.

The ancient teachings of the mysteries of the earth are probably the oldest spiritual path. In this "shamanic" wisdom that has been handed down to us from the native peoples it is taught that the earth is a living being and that the energy field of the earth and the energy fields of humans are made of the same spiritual substance. It is also believed that there are other worlds coexisting with our own in a twilight state that can be accessed by a *crack between the worlds.*

Sedona is filled with an aura of mystery that compels us to believe that there is more to life than meets the eye, and that schools do not teach all there is to know. It cannot be denied, that for whatever reason, Sedona has become *the* place people want to visit in order to try to gain a new insight or direction for their lives. I am therefore very hopeful that the meditations and information given in this book will help people have experiences that will improve their lives.

Perhaps the most important thing that can be said about the vortices of Sedona is that they inspire people to look beyond the veil of our modern world, and allow them to catch a glimpse of the world of the shaman, before the invention of science, when everything was magic.

The vortices of Sedona are not going to save the world, but our understanding of the powers that create the vortices could play a key role in helping to bring our planet into balance. There are many brilliant minds working on devices that use the energies and harmonics that are discussed in this book, which have great promise for healing the earth, but until we learn to tune into the energies of the most important vortex of all, *our hearts,* we will probably not progress.

After all my years of work and study I am now more convinced than ever, that the power of love that we find within our hearts is the greatest power we can possibly know. Love is the power of creation and it has no weaknesses. The only real path of shamanic power and illumination calls upon the infinite power of love.

Vortices come into being as an expression of universal love. There are vortices in our bodies, and vortices on our planet. We are drawn to Sedona because our bodies know that the earth's energies can help accelerate our evolution by subtly aligning our energy centers and opening them to the healing power of universal love.

This book also includes a section on my modern interpretation of the Native American medicine wheel. Anyone can use this information to build their own version of the medicine wheel, that will bring the positive energy of the earth into their home. If you use this information to create a *power spot* in your home, and you do the meditations in this book, standing in the center of your wheel, you will probably feel strong, positive energies.

Wise men, philosophers, astronomers and physicists know that everything throughout the universe is moving in a balanced harmonious dance of energy. The art and science of geomancy helps us learn to become aware of these universal energies as they are experienced upon the planet earth.

The literal meaning of the word geomancy is, "to divine the earth spirit." To "divine" is to seek understanding or knowledge through intuition. The accepted definition of geomancy, according to most modern English dictionaries is: A type of divination or fortune telling that uses features of the landscape. *The writers of the dictionary definition incorrectly assume that the "features" (forms) of the landscape are somehow "read," giving the geomancer a message.*

True geomancy is the art of using one's mind to "tune in" to the energy information matrix of the planet, thus obtaining information and guidance directly from spirit. Those who wish to perform geomantic rituals seek out power spots for an obvious reason: The energy of the earth is stronger at these places, thus making it easier to "tune in."

Geomancy is not only a type of fortune telling (becoming aware of energy as information). Geomancy is also a holistic philosophy for understanding the earth and mankind's place upon it. Geomantic philosophy assures us that we are one with the earth and that the energy of the earth is the very force from which we draw our lives.

The art of geomancy includes the performance of rituals and meditations that help the people of the earth to communicate with their planet. Group rituals are considered to be very important for maintaining planetary stability. The rituals of the modern Christian church have their origin in pagan geomantic ritual.

Those who study geomancy find that many Christian churches in Europe are built upon power spots initially identified by pagan geomancers. It is interesting to note that the word pagan originally meant that a person was a country dweller, or of the earth.

Sedona is in no way unique as a place where human beings have identified a special power or presence in the natural features of the land. Since ancient times, those who are sensitive to the spirit of nature have identified power spots such as Sedona, making them shrines or using them to conduct ceremonies which put them in touch with the Great Spirit and the spirit of the earth.

Power spots in Europe that many of our ancestors worked with were used as sites to practice a form of earth worship very similar to that of the Native American medicine wheel. These ceremonies were performed in a circle in which the four directions were always honored, and marked with a cross.

All life and matter within our planet's gravity field are part of an energy matrix that connects everything. Native American mystics speak of this as the "web of life." The Sedona vortices are just a few of the major power spots of our planet which are connected in this web of life. Strands of the web also travel through space connecting all things in the universe.

The art of geomancy is directly concerned with working with the energies of the web. Upon our earthly plane most people can best understand the web by thinking of it as Earth Energy, the biomagnetic field of the earth.

The wave pattern of our planet's biomagnetic field forms the strands of the web. These strands are known to English-speaking geomancers as ley lines. These natural lines of force connect all power spots and vortices. Some modern geomancers refer to the web as the "planetary grid."

The web acts as a group mind for the inhabitants of the planet. It is a channel for information. We seek power spots to make our special prayers because we know that these places help to amplify our prayers and project them to all other beings.

Spirit is intelligent Power - Energy is information.

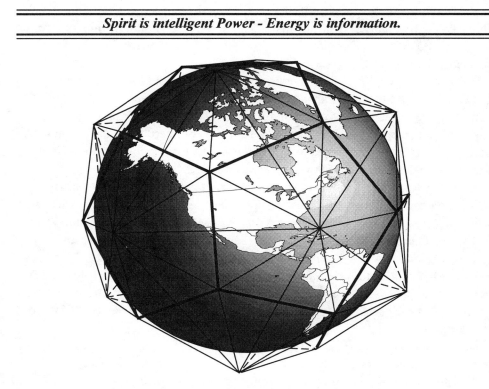

Planetary Grid System

This is the planetary grid, it is a synthesis of the platonic solids. See page 109

It is important to remember that not all shamanic techniques raise the con - sciousness or evolve the human spirit in a desirable manner. Like all mystical practices there is a path of light and a path of darkness – a path of evolution, and a path of devolution – and both paths can appear very similar to the novice. So keep it light.

Many of the beliefs, meditations and exercises detailed in this book can be regarded as forms of shamanism. True shamanism is the mystical experience of the earth spirit.

However, it is important to note that merely working with Earth Energy, or carrying a few crystals and feathers around, does not make one a shaman. The shamanic path is not as glamorous or fun as certain writers who have recently popularized this term would have us think. Those who understand the facts of shamanism know that to be a true shaman with "magical powers" is not an easy path. One must undergo trials and rigors...No one chooses to be a shaman; they are chosen "by spirit."

Like all mystical traditions, shamanism requires that the student devote a great deal of time meditating and purifying themselves so that they can become a "clear channel" for the light. This means that if you do not spend a lot of time meditating, working with crystals and otherwise improving yourself, how can you expect to be a shaman or gain any other sort psychic powers?

The average vortex explorer who reads this book should be content with simply trying to have an adventure, expand their consciousness and re-establish their mystical bond with the earth. Yes, it is common for vortex energy to trigger paranormal experiences, but experiencing past lives, mental telepathy, or interdimensional communication with "space beings" does not make one a shaman; however, any of these experiences would be a step in the right direction.

Carlos Castaneda's books contain valuable information about the mysterious possibilities and psychology of shamanic training. These teachings can also help us understand the vortex phenomenon. If you are drawn to Mr. Castaneda's work, and you feel that you understand it, then you have already begun your journey to the enchanted land.

Mr. Castaneda was a student of a Yaqui Indian "man of knowledge," whom we know as Don Juan Mateus. Don Juan traced his magical heritage to the Toltecs of Central America. In Mexico, the name "Toltecs" is synonymous with mystery, magic and art. In legend their school is said to have been founded by a man named Testatlipolca (smoking mirror).

Don Juan told Carlos that spirit had chosen him to bring the secret teachings forward so that more human beings would have the chance to escape the cycle of life and death, thus becoming beings of pure spirit. Like all schools of mystery, the path that Don Juan followed was based on the belief that *the world is an illusion which forms itself to fit the beliefs and expectations of the observer,* and that by tuning into the energy of the earth one can experience many parallel realities that coexist with our own.

4

Chapter 2

Vortices Are Windows To Infinity

Imagine a universe made of countless subatomic whiteholes and blackholes that are interdimensional gateways that allow the energy of pure spirit to manifest in space and time, thus creating all phenomena. and that every point in space is filled with these tiny vortices, which are all directly connected to the one immovable point in the universe, which is everywhere, always.

Subatomic particles are the result of these whiteholes and black-holes engaging in the practices of ecstatic un-ion. Each one of these vortices is shaped something like this:

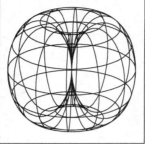

Everything in the uni-verse has a relation to this basic energy pat-tern, which we call the "torus." Toroidal en-ergy fields are formed around a vortex, an "eye of God."(Key 316:5)

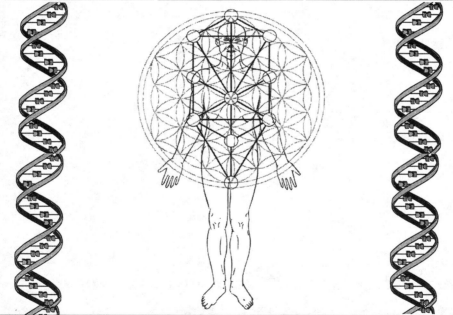

Subatomic particles are governed by the Golden Mean Proportion; together they provide the basic pattern for all creation, from light waves to DNA. These tiny torus/vortices fill the universe. The diagram above, the "Flower of Life," allows us to see how these tiny vortices fit together to create our reality. The geometry of the chemical bonds of DNA have a direct relation to the geometries of the Flower of Life, so is it any wonder that a perfectly proportioned human body could fit directly into the Flower of Life?

GENERAL THEORY OF THE FORMATION OF THE SEDONA VORTICES
The Sedona vortices are nodes in the crystallization pattern of the earth's crust.

It shall take many pages to explore the myths, theories and facts of vortex phenomenon; we begin now with simple explanations. This opening statement about the vortices is followed by several pages which explore important ideas about vortex energy and how the energy of the vortices affects our minds and bodies. Feel free to skip ahead to the section that describes the vortices themselves, but remember: in order to truly understand the vortices, you shall have to read the entire book.

Page Bryant's spiritual contacts stated that vortices of Sedona are "electromagnetic." Science tells us that EVERYTHING in the known universe is part of the electromagnetic spectrum. My own investigations have shown that electromagnetism has a direct relation to the type of life force energy that schools of yoga refer to as "Kundalini." Since ancient times this energy has often been depicted as a snake, but it certainly should not be associated with Christian ideas of evil, as Kundalini's spiral of life is an essential and primal part of the very fabric of the universe, and is life itself.

As an example of this, I will note that everything in the observable universe is rotating through time. This is a clear sign that rotation is a primal universal quality. and because everything in the known universe is also moving through time and space, rotation ALWAYS creates a spiral. The DNA molecule is the best example of the relation between time, space, rotation and life itself.

All common electrical motors, generators and older tube-type radios depend on coils (spirals) and rotating electromagnetic fields. Electromagnetism is the secondary effect of the primal energy that creates space, time, matter and life. In the English language one of the best words we have to describe this energy is "spirit," as the words spirit and spiral are derived from the Latin word for breath, which is, as we all know, essential to life.

The Sedona vortices are formed around sandstone and basalt rock formations at the edge of the Colorado Plateau. The Colorado Plateau is a monumental wave of moving slowly toward the west. Sedona is on the crest of this wave and the rock formations are the "foam." The electromagnetic field of the earth reacts with the rock, and vortices are formed as this field flows over the formations, just as water flowing in a stream creates vortices as it flows over the rocks.

Page Bryant's original channeling stated that the vortices are either "electric," "magnetic," or balanced "electromagnetic." My research and the information I have obtained from spiritual sources indicate that all of the vortices in Sedona share common qualities, and that the four vortices identified by Page's contact are not the only places around Sedona that have an odd power. Indeed, this entire area appears to share a common energy that can affect our physical and spiritual bodies, expand the consciousness and perhaps heal the body.

Electric vortices are good places for beginners to go to "get the feel." They are excellent places for work on the higher mental planes through meditation and for projecting thoughts and prayers. Electric vortices are places where the earth releases electrical energy; they are energizing. The energy boost of these vortices works directly on our bodies and indirectly upon our minds. As we increase the electrical energy within our bodies, circuits open up in our central nervous system that allow us to experience "new" levels of awareness: our psychic abilities can become awakened.

I asked the well-known channeled entity, **Kryon** about the Sedona Vortices. He said that there were many small vortices in Sedona that are part of one larger vortex. (This belief had been expressed by many people over the years.)

Kryon also stated that this primary vortex rotates counterclockwise around the valley that is bounded by Bell Rock and Cathedral Rock, and that Sedona's twin vortex was "a high, clear lake in South America," which I assume is Lake Titicaca.

Here is a simple diagram of how electromagnetic Earth Energy could be drawn into Oak Creek Canyon ① by gravity and then ejected like a fluid into Sedona, following the path of Oak Creek.

As this energy flows past Airport Hill ② it forms a natural vortex in the small canyon that separates the two hills of Airport Vortex. A certain amount of energy is carried straight up the hill, and released at the area we normally think of as Airport Vortex. The main energetic flow continues along the path of Oak Creek until it reaches Cathedral Rock, ③ where it turns toward Bell Rock. ④ This results in a large counterclockwise vortex in the valley bordered by these formations. The Chapel hills are shown at the end point. Counterclockwise vortices are expanding, could this be why the spirit of Sedona is so inspiring and unwilling to be controlled?

Magnetic vortices are perhaps even more mysterious than electrical vortices. They exist as energy fields which have no physical substance. The energies of magnetic vortices are closely associated with the etheric (non-physical) level of existence.

Magnetic vortices are excellent places for deep meditation, accessing inner levels of knowledge and contacting the "spirit of the earth." This type of vortex is also noted for its ability to trigger past-life recall and other types of paranormal experience such as telepathic communication with spirit guides. There are a number of stories about strange occurrences around Cathedral Rock, so be sure to leave yourself open to the possibilities that exist....

I feel that magnetic vortices have the ability to realign the energy field of the human body and "tune up" the aura so that it resonates properly with the energies of the earth. The subtle electrical energy current produced by a magnetic vortex may also energize the physical body on the cellular level.

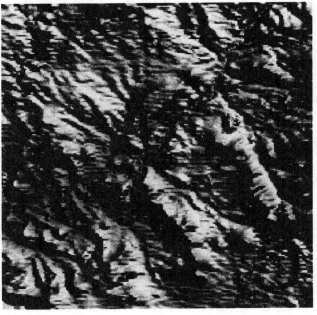

Cathedral Rock is just below the center of this image. Airport Vortex and Bell Rock are also visible. It is my theory that the vortices are the natural result of the quantum forces that govern the formation of the earth's crust.

In the center of this satellite image you can see that numerous contours in the landscape converge into a node at Cathedral Rock. Oak Creek also cuts through the middle of this image. The spot where it makes its abrupt turn toward the west is directly in the middle of this image.

Most people can easily feel the current of Earth Energy that flows with the waters that pass by the foot of this formation but will never have the chance to hike to the "saddle" between the towers. If you do decide to climb to the saddle, I suggest that you do not head up from the creek side, as this route is far more difficult than the eastern route that starts at "Back O' Beyond." See maps

BOYNTON CANYON, THE "ELECTROMAGNETIC" VORTEX

The Apache Indians who lived in the red rock country before the arrival of the Europeans considered Boynton Canyon to be a sacred place, and believed that there was a powerful feminine earth spirit living in the canyon. Today's Apache also believe that the first woman of their tribe lived in this canyon.

Page Bryant's original channeling stated that the Boynton Canyon Vortex is a balanced combination of electrical and magnetic energies. I think that the point of balance for these energies in the canyon is the formation that adjoins the Enchantment Resort on the west side.

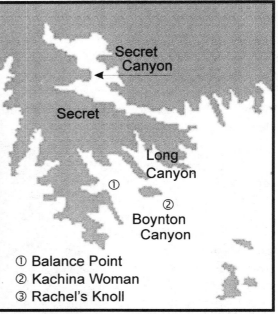

This formation is on a node where the branches of Boynton Canyon converge. My favorite exercise for feeling the energy that circulates around this formation is to go into the canyon late in the afternoon in the middle of summer, just after the sun goes down over the ridge, and walk very quietly and gently along the trail, immersing myself in the meditation of just walking and *feeling*. I find that this sometimes allows me to catch a glimmer of the enchanted landscape.

The easiest place to feel Earth Energy in Boynton Canyon is around the Kachina Woman formation on the descending ridge east of the Forest Service parking lot. It is an easy hike, but be sure to follow the trail that starts near the sign-in box.

I have seen a number of photographs taken in the area of the Kachina Woman formation at the entrance to Boynton Canyon that have a blue aura in them that I suspect is caused by the electromagnetic forces that create the vortices. Descending ridgelines are apparently discharge points for these energies. Each of Sedona's descending ridges seem to have a Rock spire that has a geometrical relation to the Kachina Woman, as if they were fractals of one another.

Secret Mountain separates Boynton Canyon and Secret Canyon. The "Secret" underground base that I refer to in the UFO section of this book is somewhere in the vicinity of the area where Secret Canyon coils around Secret Mountain, just north of Boynton Canyon.

1. Everything within our planetary sphere is part of a common field of energy that links all things together. The human mind, body and spirit share a common resonance with the planetary energy field.

2. Our planet's energy field is influenced by the three key elements that also make up most of our planet's mass: iron, silicon and oxygen. This planet's magnetic field is produced by iron as it reacts with the dimension of pure potential.

3. It is these three elements which make up much of the red Rock formations in Sedona, and it should be understood that these sandstone and basalt formations have definite electronic qualities.

4. Science tells us that our bloodstream carries many magnetized particles of iron oxide (magnetite). The membrane in front of the pituitary gland (one of our organs of psychic awareness in the brain) also contains magnetite crystals. Given these facts, we should begin to see that there is a common resonance between these elements in our blood, our brains and the red rocks themselves.

5. Sedona is at the edge of the Colorado Plateau, which is essentially a huge wave of Rock moving slowly toward the west. The formations of Sedona are the "foam" at the crest of the wave. The Rock formations react with the earth's electromagnetic field and create natural vortices, in a manner similar to water flowing over rocks in a stream.

6. It is interesting to note that one of Dick Sutphen's students noticed that "Sedona" spelled backward is "anodes," which is an electrical term for the positive plate in a vacuum tube and the negative plate in a battery. The original Greek root for the word anode is "anodos," which translates into English as "a way up." I am convinced that meditating around any of the monumental Rock spires around Sedona does indeed elevate one's consciousness.

7. Small amounts of electrical energy are released into the atmosphere at the earth's surface; this is known as the *corona discharge effect*. The corona discharge along high points of the earth's surface is greater than that of level ground. The sandstone spires in the Sedona area are ideal discharge points for electrical energy from the earth.

8. Some of this electrical energy reacts with oxygen in the air, thus forming negative ions. These ions energize the body as we breathe them in. Electrons carry a negative charge that energizes, and protons carry a positive charge that binds.

9. Vortex energy is also a form of spirit – intelligent energy – a connection with the creative forces of the universe.

When we speak of a vortex of Earth Energy as being either electrical or magnetic, we are not only referring to the presence of electromagnetic energy; we are also speaking of a place where the very fabric of the universe is distorted in a manner that allows power from the dimension of pure energy to "leak through" into our dimension. *Every magnetized iron atom is an interdimensional portal that creates a magnetic field by bringing the power of pure spirit into the physical dimension.*

The words "electricity" and "magnetism" help our logical minds begin to grasp the forces of universal creation that form our world. We are, however, missing the point if we always insist on describing the forces we encounter at the vortices with the terms we use to describe ordinary reality.

True mystics know that the only way to truly understand the energies of spirit is to go beyond definitions. We must use our powers of meditation to help us see beyond the veil and experience spirit directly.

Many people who work with the vortices believe that the strongest component of the vortex exists not on the physical plane but on the astral and etheric planes. Anything we detect as being either electric or magnetic is actually a secondary effect of a much more profound force that exists in the realm of spirit.

A vortex is a place where the energies of the spiritual realm are entering the physical. When we "tune in" to the energy of a vortex, our minds and bodies are able to learn of spirit directly from spirit: energy is information (Jose Argüelles).

Simply meditating anywhere also helps us learn directly from spirit. Remember that spirit is the force from which our world is woven; it is with us at all times. When we quiet our minds and "go within" we learn the lessons of spirit.

THE SYMBOL OF INTERDIMENSIONAL REALITY

Since ancient times we have used symbols to help our logical minds grasp metaphysical truths that are beyond the limits of ordinary reality. It is from the ancients we get this symbol and the teaching that our world coincides with another realm: the realm of pure spirit.

The two interlocking circles represent the world of spirit and the world of physical reality. The center part of this glyph represents the "crack between the worlds," the vortex through which energy flows between the two realms.

This overlapping of the worlds is happening on many levels, and it is in fact impossible for our three-dimensional minds to fully comprehend how these things work. True understanding comes through the experiences gained by meditation and the direct experience of spirit that meditation brings.

Scientists tell us that the entire universe is a unified field of energy; every square inch of space – even the pure vacuum of deep space – is full of energy. Magnetism is a secondary effect of this field of pure energy as it interacts with matter. Magnetic energy has no substance; it exists as a non-physical "field."

For many years scientists believed that there was an element or dimension through which energies, such as light and radio waves traveled in, or *originated from*. This dimension was referred to as "aether," or "ether." The concept of ether was "borrowed" from the ancient schools of the mysteries by Renaissance scien- tists who based their scientific theories upon a mystical view of the universe.

Theories based upon the existence of ether were popular among scientists until the 1920s. Modern physicists no longer base their theories upon the exis- tence of ether; instead they prefer to say that there are at least ten dimensions parallel to our own.

A student of metaphysics may casually refer to the dimensions of pure energy as "ether." The phrase "etheric plane" is often used as a generic term to describe the entire spectrum of "energy realms" (dimensions) which co-exist side by side with our own three-dimensional time-space reality. Often we refer to things (such as the human aura) as being on the "etheric plane."

As metaphysicians, we know that magnetic fields and electrical energy are manifestations of pure life force on the physical plane, and that the electromag- netic phenomenon of the physical plane draws its energy from the universal source that exists in the non-physical "ether" (the realm of spirit).

Iron produces magnetic fields of seemingly limitless duration because it is ca- pable of tapping into the universal field of energy (which exists on the etheric plane, side by side with our own reality), and changing that energy into a magnetic field. (This is known as transduction. Quartz crystals are also energy transducers.)

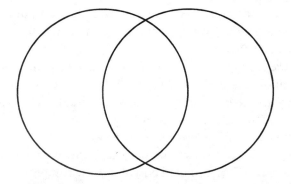

The Aharonov-Bohm effect indicates that the space that surrounds us is filled by an energy field that is more "...fundamental than electric or magnetic fields."
See Scientific American, April 1989, page 56, for more information.

Vortex energy is sometimes referred to as "psychic energy." This is because we know that the electromagnetic Earth Energy of the vortices is capable of stimulating our minds in a manner that triggers "psychic phenomena," events that can be considered to be "paranormal" (beyond the "normal" experience of life).

The human body is "tuned" to the electromagnetic field of the earth. When we allow ourselves to relax, our minds automatically tune in to what is known as the earth wave.

It is a scientific fact that the stability of our bodily functions is dependent upon the electronic stimulation of our planet's electromagnetic field. This was proven by NASA scientists in the mid 1960s.

The first Astronauts to go into orbit became mysteriously ill but soon recovered upon returning to earth. NASA scientists speculated that the astronauts had become ill because they had been deprived of the stimulation of the earth's electromagnetic field.

This was later proven when the astronaut's metabolism remained stable after a low power transmitter was placed in the space capsule to create an artificial electromagnetic field that pulsed at 7.83 cycles per second.

NASA scientists named the wave that occurs between 7-8 cps: the "earth wave." Please note that the theta brain wave state, which is associated with deep sleep, relaxation and meditation also, occurs between 7-8 cps. Therefore, when we relax and meditate, we are resonating with the earth wave.

The earth wave, or "Schumann resonance," was first detected by Nicola Tesla in the early 1900's. It is the result of an average of two thousand lightning strikes per minute worldwide and the electrical resonance between the ionosphere and the surface of the earth. Various New Age sources have claimed the frequency of the Schumann resonance is increasing, but records maintained over the past 100 years indicate that is not correct.

Before negative ions or earth waves were ever heard of, those who wanted to develop their mental abilities were encouraged to do things that naturally increase the body's electrical potential.

Students on the spiritual path are always encouraged to do breathing exercises. These exercises allow the body to absorb increased amounts of electrical energy from the air. They also help the body balance and circulate its energy.

Those who want to experience higher levels of consciousness are also encouraged to drink pure water, and eat live healthy foods which are known to be "full of life force." Live foods carry desirable electrical energy to the body. Processed foods, carbonated beverages rob the body of electrical energy.

The "psychic energy" of the vortices has a direct relation to electrical energy . When our bodies' full electrical potential is reached, our mental abilities are increased.

THE TORUS

The Torus is the most common form of energy field.

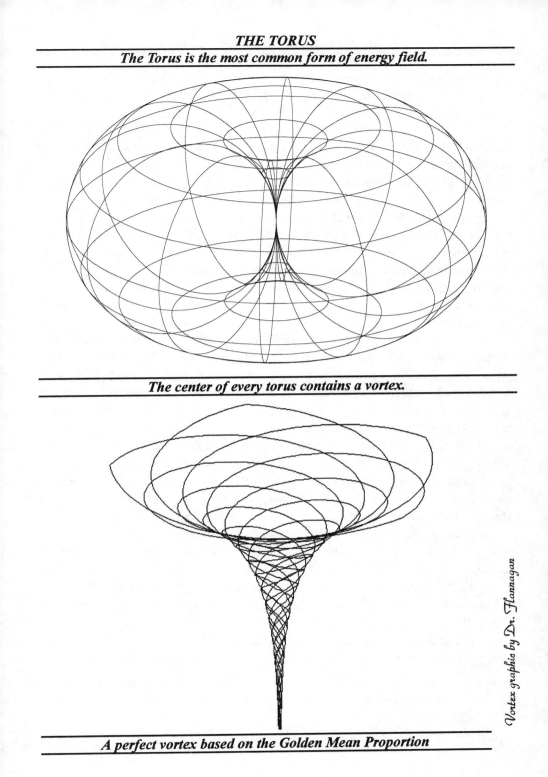

The center of every torus contains a vortex.

A perfect vortex based on the Golden Mean Proportion

Vortex graphic by Dr. Flannagan

or

THE FRACTAL NATURE OF REALITY AND THE "UNIVERSAL FRACTAL."

A fractal is a system that contains multiple discrete units that contain all the information needed to recreate the entire system. In the study of sacred geometry we are told that all the information to construct the universe is contained in the relatively simple forms known as the Platonic Solids, which are in turn governed by a mathematic ratio of 1:618.... We call this the Golden Mean Proportion.

Science has confirmed that the basic energy patterns of our universe often conform to the Golden Mean Proportion. Dr. Alex Kaivarainen* has also developed an exciting theoretical model for the formation of matter from sub-atomic particles that, when brought down into the simplest terms, demonstrates that the most basic building blocks of our reality are governed by the ratio of 1:168... and that everything else is a fractal of this ratio. It is from this discovery that I get the phrase "universal fractal."

This proportion is the basic pattern for the formation of perfect vortices. Dan Winter's research demonstrates how a torus modeled in Golden Mean proportions will produce 3-D wave patterns that turn inside out perfectly, in perfect proportion, and that an infinite number of these waves would fit within one another perfectly. The Golden Mean Proportion produces a perfect vortex; therefore, *the vortex itself is a basic quality inherent in all creation.*

Dr. Henri Coanda, an important pioneer of fluid dynamics, discovered that a vortex is formed along the edges of the wings of aircraft, and that this was what creates *lift.* Dr. Coanda became an expert in vortex mechanics and proposed that natural vortices in rivers and streams may achieve center velocities close to the speed of light, which to a scientist or a metaphysician, is very exciting.

Arthur Young, inventor of the original Bell helicopter, had a keen interest in physics and metaphysics. He noted that particles such as electrons and protons are toroidal, and that the curvature of space-time is also probably toroidal. He also noted that the mathematic formula for calculating the volume and surface of a torus had a direct relation to the formulas used in quantum theory. Therefore, it is safe to theorize that the universe is a torus!**

The center of a torus is a vortex; therefore, the energy pattern of the vortex is inherent throughout all space and time. This is what the yogis call Kundalini.

* Dr. Alex Kaivarainen, Petrozavodsk State University, Department of Applied Mathematics and Cybernetics, Leading Scientist, Ph.D., D. Sc. (Physics & Biophysics); Adjunct Professor of University of Miami, Chem. Dept. (USA)

    http://www.karelia.ru/~alexk/   h2o@karelia.ru   alexk@kftt.karelia.ru
** Arthur Young, Reflexive Universe

The Fibonacci and Golden Mean Spirals As The Primary Energy Patterns For All Vortex Formation

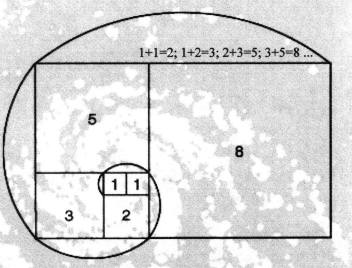

1+1=2; 1+2=3; 2+3=5; 3+5=8 ...

5

8

1 1

3 2

The Fibonacci and Golden Mean spirals are almost identical to one another.

The Golden Mean ratio, 1:618... is found throughout nature.

The Fibonacci set describes the Golden Mean ratio in whole numbers.

This sequence consists of simple addition, beginning with 1+1.
1+1=2; 1+2=3; 2+3=5; 3+5=8; 5+8=13; 8+13=21; 13+21=34; 21+34=55; 34+55=89; 55+89=144, etc. to infinity. (144 is the 12th number in the sequence.)

Chapter 3

The Land of Enchantment

I encourage you to study the maps in this book.

When you arrive in Sedona, check notices on the various bulletin boards at the crystal shops and book stores around town. Attending the events or ceremonies which are advertised upon these bulletin boards is an excellent way to get in contact with the locals.

When you get to Sedona you will want to drive around and look things over. But please remember that you cannot do everything in a couple of days. In fact, if you try to do too much, you may find that by the end of your stay you have accomplished very little.

Those who rush around from place to place are missing the point entirely. After you have looked things over, it is important to settle down and do one thing at a time. Remember that you came here seeking spiritual insight, so don't forget to spend time quietly meditating outside.

Plan to spend full days, or half days at one area. Bring some food, water and a working flashlight, (in case you get caught out after dark). Always try to stick around and watch the sunset. You can usually get back to your car before it gets dark.

After you have become familiarized with the Sedona area, I suggest that you focus on getting in touch with just a few places that are special to you. So instead of running around wondering what to do, you always have special places that you are familiar with that you can return to time after time.

You can choose a quiet spot off the beaten trail where you can do some serious meditating. Or for fun, you could set up camp right beside a trail somewhere and talk to the people who come along. This can be quite entertaining, and you never know who you might meet.

Here in Sedona we hike all year round. It is never too hot or too cold for hardy individuals to venture out, and there are several months each year of moderate temperatures which everyone finds quite agreeable. But remember, midday summer temperatures can easily reach 100°F, so remember to wear a hat and some sunscreen and take plenty of water along. A wise adventurer may decide to explore during the mornings, the late afternoon and evenings, staying someplace cool during the hot part of the day.

During warm months I suggest that you get up early and hike in the mornings; the air and the light can be fantastic! If you work up a sweat in the afternoon, perhaps you might like to head for the creek for a swim. Afternoon naps by the creekside are proven methods of rejuvenation. *Do not drink creek water! Too many people live along the creek, and the bacteria count can get rather high.* (Don't worry if you get a few drops in your mouth, it probably will not hurt you.)

Fall and spring have both warm and cool days, but it is important to remember that a warm afternoon can give way to a rather cool evening, so be prepared! During the fall and spring it is a good idea to always set out on a hike with a sweater or light jacket in your daypack. Always carry water and something to snack on. (Dried fruit, such as figs or dates, make excellent trail food.)

Whatever season it is, during cloudy weather it is a good idea to stay of out narrow canyons and to keep to the high ground. Arizona is flash flood country. Rainstorms several miles away can send deadly walls of water down canyons and gullies. Some of the heaviest rainfalls occur in late July, August and September, so watch it.

It is a good idea to check local conditions before going hiking or camping. A simple phone call to the Sedona ranger station is all it takes to find out about weather conditions or fire restrictions.

Always avoid "going to the bathroom" near steams, springs and wells. This is one of the reasons the water in Oak Creek is not safe to drink. Decomposing human waste creates bacteria that is deadly to human beings. Solid human waste should always be buried about ten inches below the soil. If it is not, it be - comes both a health hazard and a rather unsightly landmark.

Snakes hide out and hunt in the bushes. Knowing this fact should give you a good reason to stay on the trail. The other good reason for staying on the trail is that if you go off the trail you are probably damaging plants. The plants are living things and deserve respect. They also hold the soil, thus preventing erosion.

When many people visit the same area and they do not stay on the trails, the native plants get torn up. As you visit power spots such as Bell Rock and the Airport vortices, notice how many plants have been damaged by careless hikers. The excessive damage to plants in these areas is simply pathetic, **so please stay on the trail.**

It is especially important to stay on the trails in the spring time. This is the time when the grasses and weeds are first sprouting and they are very tender. These small plants are very important. They prevent erosion. If they get stomped early in the spring, the patch of soil in which they were hoping to take root may get washed away.

People with dogs should take note: Dogs frequently turn out to be a real nuisance while on trips. Rattlesnakes are rough on dogs, and city dogs often run off after rabbits, or some other thing, and are hard to get back (if at all). Rabbits, and all other rodents in the Southwest may have disease-carrying fleas or ticks. This is no joke. Often, the best thing to do is to leave Rover home.

NEVER HANDLE ANY RODENTS (especially wild rabbits).

If you want to find the interesting places, just follow the trails.

The best way to find the trail is to start from the place where people usually park their cars. Look down at the ground, if there is a trail there you will be able to see a ribbon of bare earth leading in between the bushes. Usually, there will also be footprints.

Sometimes when you get to a place where the trail "branches off" or is indistinct, the best route will often be marked with a small pile of stones. These small piles are placed there by people who want to help you find the way, so keep your eyes open for little piles of stone or ribbons tied into tree branches.

Typically, if you miss the trail you will end up walking for a little way only to find that the brush is getting thicker and thicker. You will either have to go crashing through the brush to get back on the right trail, or you will have to backtrack.

Crashing through the brush is a not a good practice. You can get scratched or tear your clothes, and it is also hard on the bushes. Snakes can also be encountered in the bushes. So please stay on the trail. Every time a person goes crashing through the bushes they break off some branches. Trees and bushes around here grow slowly, so every little twig or branch counts. Damage to the forest is cumulative; over the period of years things can really get torn up.

Pay careful attention to your footing while you are on steep trails and mountainsides. Keep your hands out of your pockets, and your eyes upon the trail!

Occasionally I meet someone who claims they were lost in one of the Canyons, his is a bit silly as there are only two ways you can go: up (in) or down (out), and a person is not really lost until someone back home notices they are missing.

If you ever get confused, stop and think for a moment. In a canyon, you can either go up (in) or down (out). Look at your surroundings. You should be able to tell which way the ground is sloping. Usually, while in the Sedona area, as we leave our cars and go into the canyons, we are going up. So if we want to get back to our cars we should go down. Right?

You can also look for "landmarks." These are things such as trees, rocks and mountains that we remember seeing on the trail or in the distance.

As you go along, make mental notes of landmarks which catch your eye, such as: "We turned when we got to this burned tree." Or you might take note of a mountain in the distance, and later in the day, as you make your way back to your car, you might think: "That mountain was behind me as I walked off from my car, so now I should walk toward that mountain to find my car."

The only people I have ever known to have serious problems hiking in Sedona are strong young men who climb alone. Sometimes it has taken months to find their remains. If you stay on the popular trails there is very little chance of getting lost or hurt.

Life has many hazards. One should not allow fear to control their life but should be aware that the further they venture from their bed, the more the potential for bodily harm increases.

I know a woman who fell off a cliff while hiking with friends here and was almost killed while her friends watched. She broke several bones, got a concussion and cracked a vertebra in her back.

I bet she thought she was doing just fine a split second before whatever she was standing on gave way. Fortunately for her, she made a miraculous recovery and is enjoying great health today (a rough way to get initiated, or so they say).

BE CAREFUL! The Sedona landscape has many hazards.

DISCLAIMER

YOU ARE INVITED TO READ THE FINE PRINT

The author, the publisher, the Vortex Society and Sedona Information Services do not specifically recommend that anyone hike or engage in any hazardous activities.

The author, the publisher, the Vortex Society and Sedona Information Services accept no responsibility for damages that might be incurred as a result of engaging in any of the physical, ceremonial or spiritual exercises detailed in this manual. People suffering from mental disorders, epilepsy or fundamentalism are advised to refrain from engaging in any of the aforementioned exercises and practices.

A friend of mine who used to work for a tour company told me that I shouldn't even mention snakes, because it scares people. He said that in all the time he had been in Sedona, he had never seen a rattlesnake, so why should I scare people with snake stories? The answer to this is simple: Don't be frightened, be aware.

Snakes tend to avoid places where they encounter people. Popular vortices and well-used trails are usually snake free. Isolated areas such as the back of Long Canyon are places where you had better be careful.

The best way to avoid snakebite is to be aware of the times when they are out and to KEEP YOUR EYES OPEN! Look where you are walking! and stay on the trail at all times! Do not walk through bushes.

Warm summer nights are times when the snakes are out. (Keep your eyes and your nose out for skunks too.) Use a flashlight to guide your steps, and try to avoid sleeping on the ground without a tent. Snakes are heat seekers and they have been known to follow people into their sleeping bags. You should also be aware of the fact that scorpions have this same nasty habit of cuddling up with people at night; they also like to hide in shoes and boots. So always shake out your shoes and your clothes before you put them on. Scorpion bites are very seldom deadly.

Day or night, you will never encounter a snake if it is cold. Snakes are cold blooded and they hibernate when it is cold. During fall and spring, on warm afternoons you might encounter snakes sunning themselves on rocks.

Doctors advise those who are bitten by a snake to leave the wound alone and seek medical attention. **Remain as calm as possible**; snakebite victims have been known to become badly overexcited, thus making matters much worse. Anti-venom is supposedly effective for up to three hours after a bite. However, no one is going to waste any time getting to a hospital.

If someone gets bitten by a snake, try to capture it, or at least try to remember what it looks like. This information is helpful in finding the right anti-venom. Don't panic. Find a phone, dial 911, and ask which clinic to go to. At the time of this writing, there is an emergency medical clinic in West Sedona, but the only hospital in this area is in Cottonwood, which is about twenty miles west of Sedona.

I am told the **old Indian cure** for snakebite was to drink one's own urine immediately after being bitten. Science tells us this may be valid, as this may replace hydrogen ions that can neutralize the venom.

MORE SNAKEBITE FACTS:

Twenty-five percent of all known "single strike" snakebites are "dry"... no venom is injected. (But don't let 'em bite twice.) A snake that appears dead can still bite.

The desert grasslands of Sedona are often quite dry. Please be very careful with your fires, and please respect seasonal fire restrictions.

I seldom build a fire when I camp. I find that if I have a fire, I tend to stare at it. Not only is this bad for the eyes, it keeps the happy camper from fully experiencing what the night is really like. Oh yes, you might look at the stars for a few minutes, but you will always end up staring at the fire.

To cook only takes a very small fire, a so-called "pocket fire." A fire like this can be made very quickly and easily from small twigs gathered from the ground near your camp. With a small fire it is easy to do things such as boil water and pop corn because you can easily control the heat.

I find that two or three head-sized (or smaller) rocks, with the fire in between, works well for most cooking. You can put your pot on top of the crack between the rocks and feed the twigs in from the side. This type of fire is also easy to put out, therefore, it is less of a fire hazard.

FIRES ARE NO LONGER PERMITTED OUTSIDE CAMPGROUNDS

Always build fires away from brush, and never under or near a tree. Remember that wind can carry sparks many feet into dry brush, and that large fires can reach out, or up, to set nearby trees on fire. Roots in the ground below fires can also be fire hazards. They can be caught on fire and slowly "burn back" into a dead tree, starting a fire long after the campers are gone.

If you must have a fire, it is a good idea to bring your own wood. Do not attack the trees! Remember that you are in the land of enchantment and trees are often inhabited by earth spirits. I would also like you to take special notice of the trees when you are out and about. Often times a gnarly tree marks a power spot.

On nights when there is little or no moonlight, the stars can look very intense, and after you have been in the full darkness for awhile, you should actually be able to see fairly well. In fact many people who have never really experienced the outdoors in the nighttime are amazed at how well they can see after their eyes become adjusted!

Whenever you go out at night it is of course always a good idea to have a good working flashlight. Small flashlights which fit in the pocket or on a key ring can be amazingly powerful.

On nights when the moon is bright you can usually see well enough to walk quite safely without the aid of a flashlight. Unless it is snake season.

Some people take going out into the dark of the night quite naturally. They put aside their childhood fears of darkness and learn to trust spirit.

Chapter 4

Sedona's Places Of Power

SCHEMATIC MAP OF THE SEDONA AREA

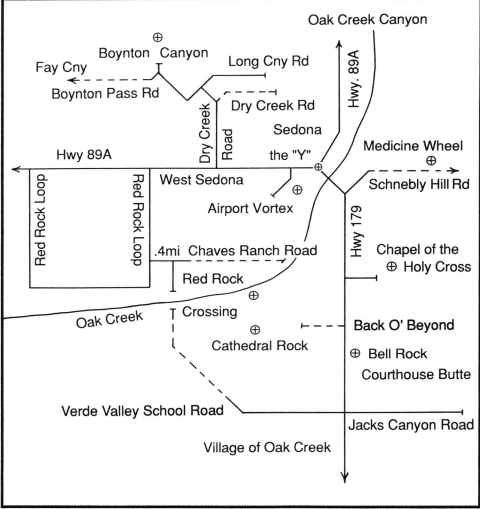

Oak Creek Canyon

Boynton Canyon

Fay Cny

Long Cny Rd

Boynton Pass Rd

Dry Creek Rd

Hwy. 89A

Dry Creek Road

Sedona
the "Y"

Medicine Wheel

Hwy 89A

West Sedona

Schnebly Hill Rd

Red Rock Loop

Red Rock Loop

Airport Vortex

Hwy 179

.4mi Chaves Ranch Road

Chapel of the
⊕ Holy Cross

Red Rock

Oak Creek

Crossing

Back O' Beyond

Cathedral Rock

⊕ Bell Rock

Courthouse Butte

Verde Valley School Road

Jacks Canyon Road

Village of Oak Creek

Please note that this map is not to scale, it shows only major roads, intersections, and places of interest. — All distances are from the "Y" - the intersection of highways 179 and 89a. All mileage figures are approximate. — Straight solid lines are paved roads, broken lines are dirt roads.

AIRPORT VORTEX - 1 mile. Take highway 89a West. Turn left at Airport Road. Go up the hill until you have passed the last house on the left. Park in any one of the parking areas. Always off the road!

BELL ROCK - 5.5 miles. Take highway 179 South 5.5 miles.

BOYNTON CANYON - 7.75 miles. Take highway 89a West to Dry Creek Road (3 miles) turn right. After 3 miles you will be at the intersection of Dry Creek and Long Canyon roads, turn left. Go 1.6 miles to next crossroad turn right. The parking lot for Boynton Canyon is less than half a mile from this last intersection.

CATHEDRAL ROCK - 4.2 miles. Take highway 179 East 3.2 miles to Back O' Beyond road. Turn right. Parking lot 1 mile.

Map of Sedona

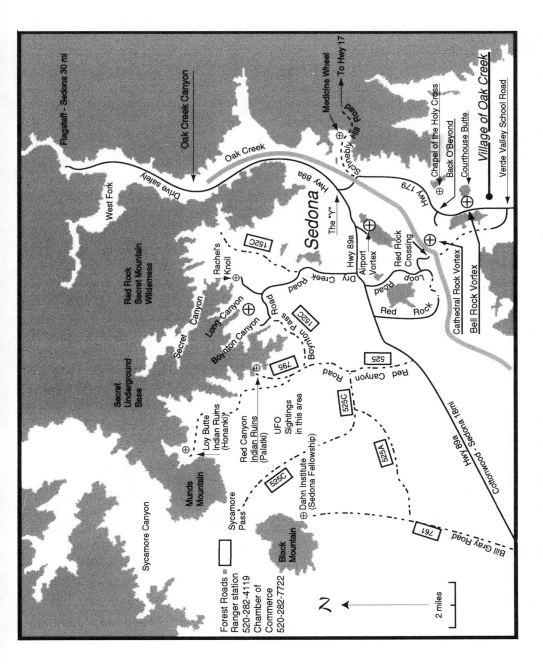

There are many beautiful and quiet spots along Oak Creek.

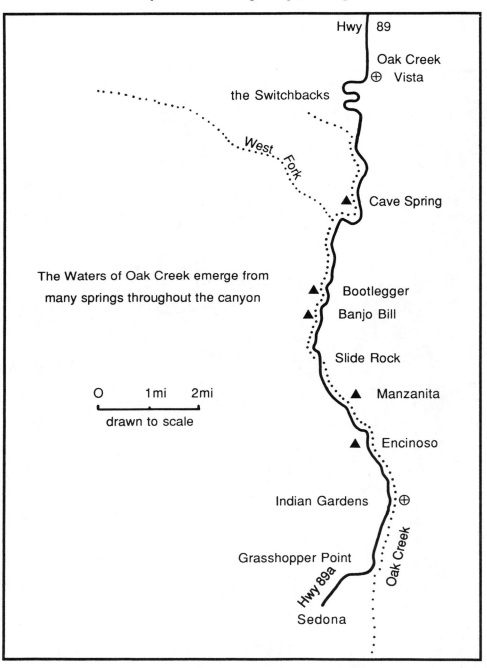

A visit to Oak Creek may be the most healing experience that the Red Rock Country has to offer. Simply relaxing and letting go of our problems can be far more beneficial to our health and happiness than visiting a vortex or power spot.

Shaman's and mystics often spend a great deal of time clearing their thoughts before they attempt to work with power. They know that when they open themselves up and become a channel for spirit, their Intent has to be clear or else there may be problems.

Before we visit a vortex or other power spot, we need to relax and let go of our troubles. Not only can our negative emotions become amplified and projected back out into the energy field of the planet, but these energies can also pollute the energies of the power spots as well.

WATER IS SACRED, WATER IS LIFE

Quiet spots along the creek are ideal places for spiritual, emotional and mental rejuvenation. Healing currents of Earth Energy are found where water flows freely upon the earth.

Water has been well known for ages as being very sacred and healing, not just to the body, but to the soul. Always respect places of water; we are born of water, and we are water. The Master Jesus was baptized in water. That baptism was more than symbolic; it was a cleansing of the aura.

It is not always necessary to actually get into water to benefit from its healing powers. Just spending time near the water can be healing, especially if a person goes there with the intent of letting go of their problems.

FIVE MEDITATIONS FOR THE CREEKSIDE

1. Do a color meditation. Concentrate upon the green color of the trees, breathe in the color with each breath. Green is the color which stimulates the heart chakra. This exercise is both energizing and energy balancing. (See both the Airport Vortex section and the color meditation section for more information about this type of meditation.)
2. Listen to the water with your eyes closed; concentrate upon sensing nothing but this sound – the song of God. This meditation balances the left and right side of the brain.
3. Watch the water. As each thought comes into your mind, let it go into the water.
4. Lie upon the sand, the soil, or a comfortable rock and feel your connection with the earth. This exercise can be done lying upon your back, or lying face down. If you do this exercise lying face down you may have the distinct sensation that energy from your solar plexus is moving down into the earth and merging with the energy of the mother. If you put your forehead to the earth, you may feel that you can actually project your consciousness into the rocks. This exercise is very healing, and "grounding."
5. While you are in the water, concentrate upon feeling its healing energy.

Courthouse Butte is the formation a few hundred feet east of Bell Rock. Due to a mapmaker's error in the 1920s, Courthouse Butte is often confused with the formation near the creek at Red Rock Crossing, called Cathedral Rock. Old Timers will tell you that these two formations are "named backwards." This mis-naming continues to be a source of confusion. For the sake of clarity this guide book uses the names for these two formations as they appear in "official" Forest Service maps.

From many locations around the Sedona area we can see that the entire summit of Courthouse Butte appears to form a silhouette of a human face staring skyward. This monumental image awakens our sense of mystery and mythology, beckoning those with a sense of adventure to explore beyond the "veil."

We know that the shapes of the Rock formations of Sedona are constantly changing and that we can see many figures in these rocks. Someday the face on Courthouse Butte will be gone. But for those of us who are here today, who are drawn to Sedona to learn the ways of the earth, this face is a sign that the spirit of the earth resides in the red rocks. It is a symbol of the mythos and the mystical, mysterious, enchanted landscape that exists on the other side of reality's veil.

Pay careful attention to your dreams while you are in Sedona. The spirit of the earth often communicates with us through our dreams. These "power dreams" form a link between our conscious mind, the native awareness of the body, and the spirit of the earth.

Many people who are interested in re-establishing their connection with the earth feel a mysterious primal bond with the Native Americans and their culture. This connection with the past draws many people to the ruins of ancient native dwellings. I cannot caution the reader enough to always treat these places with respect: Take no souvenirs, move no stones, leave nothing behind.

The picture above is of a cliff that has two alcoves in it which are typical of places in which "Indian ruins" are found. If you are hiking in a canyon and see alcoves that appear to have ruins in them, and you would like to visit them, look for a trail that branches off the main trail and seems to head in the direction you want to go.

If there is anything interesting in the direction you want to go, there will be a trail, but please be aware that there are also many trails in the canyons that come to a dead end, so if your trail suddenly ends, please do not try going through the brush; you should instead backtrack to the main trail and try again.

It can be quite inspiring to find even a very small trace of an ancient dwelling. Artifacts like this help us understand who we are, and where we came from. There are hundreds of so-called archaeological sites in the Sedona area. These sites may simply be small piles of rubble, or extensive structures such as Montezuma's Castle and Tuzigoot. (Both of which are maintained by the National Park Service; **check your maps.** Montezuma's Castle is near Montezuma's Well – a few miles south of Sedona). The ruins shown on the main map now charge $5 per person, and the Forest Service is also campaigning for toll fees for using their roads.

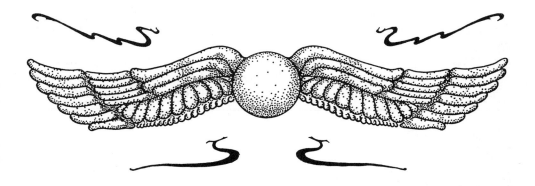

When you are have become "well-tuned" by meditating on the energies of the earth, it is an excellent time to activate your psychic center with a crystal.... Place a quartz crystal to your forehead, and focus upon that place known as the "third eye"...If you have the right crystal you should feel an energy sensa- tion when you apply it to your forehead... your psychic awareness center is be- ing activated.... Beginners should not do this for more than about fifteen seconds, or it may "overload" your circuits.

Working with the energy of Bell Rock can be a catalyst that removes blockages in your personal energy field and opens your psychic centers. After your meditation at this vortex you will hopefully continue to experience subtle changes that lead to higher levels of consciousness and increased psychic abilities.

Bell Rock is an electric vortex. Its energy can be energizing and usually has positive effects, such as a heightened state of awareness.

The subtle electrical stimulation of the Bell Rock Vortex creates an aura of ex - citement, mystery and adventure that has inspired visitors for hundreds of years. The Apache Indians who are native to this area were very much aware of Bell Rock's qualities and have a traditional teaching that Bell Rock is a place of the Ea - gle Spirit thus associating this vortex with the sun, spiritual upliftment and the pri - mal creative power of the universe.

I feel that the most important qualities of the Sedona vortices are that they can help us tune in to our natural ability to work with spirit, and that this energy can also be used to clear undesirable thoughtforms. The energy of a powerful vortex such as this brings us into closer contact with the infinite power of God, and most people who use the techniques given in this book should be able to get an energetic boost from this vortex and a glimmering of interdimensional awareness.

I think I have a pretty good idea how the Bell Rock Vortex came into being. To visualize this it is important to understand that the rock formations of Sedona are always changing. and while the rocks may seem very solid, they actually flow very slowly, like a fluid. Over a period of hundreds of millions of years the sandstone has been carried across the continent with water, "frozen" into solid rock, and once again melted away by wind and rain, thus creating the complex formations we see today.

From a math and physics-based perspective, the rock formations of Sedona are like the foam at the edge of a wave breaking on a beach. This foam is a complex pattern of wave harmonics. All the formations in Sedona are part of this phenome - non, but Bell Rock happens to be a particularly important node where the waves come together to form a strong vortex. This is even reflected in the shape of Bell Rock itself, as it does resemble a classic funnel-shaped conical vortex.

When I meditate on Bell Rock I receive an image similar to DNA, in that I per - ceive two separate counter-rotating streams of energy spiraling around the forma - tion, and that both of these streams converge to create an interdimensional window above the formation where energy flows in and out of the vortex .

In the past, various channels have claimed that aliens use Bell Rock as some type of portal. I cannot say whether this is true or not, but over the years I have received odd letters from people claiming that they have ob - served "aliens" in the area. I would like to believe that some of these stories are true (as long as they are well-behaved aliens), but if any beings have the power to travel to earth from other star systems, I would hope that they did not need the help of a large piece of sandstone. Who knows? Perhaps they just like the scenery.

I have worked with the energy of the Bell Rock for a number of years and have found that this energy can facilitate powerful altered states of consciousness. The meditation described here is a metaphysical exercise that increases the meditator's strength and abilities. This type of meditation has been known to trigger paranormal experiences which frequently have a positive transformational effect upon the psyche.

This meditation is a spiraling energy meditation. Please read the meditation section of this book for more details on spiraling energy meditations and the pillar of light.

This meditation alters the energy pattern of the body. Those who have read Carlos Castaneda's books, particularly the *Eagle's Gift, The Fire Within*, and *The Power of Silence,* will perhaps have an easier time understanding the hows, and whys of the "energy shift" which is referred to in these books as "shifting the point of awareness."

This meditation can be done either sitting or standing. As usual, you should practice calming yourself with regular breathing before you actually begin.

Establish your connection with the earth by giving yourself mental instructions to "become connected with the earth."

Focus your Intent on "tuning in" to the energy of the vortex. After a few minutes of meditation many people will be able to feel this energy flow.

Say these words out loud; **"I am connected to the earth, our energies flow together."** Use your "mind's eye" to visualize energy flowing both in and out of the energy center (chakra) at the base of your spine, and through the soles of your feet. Visualize yourself as an energy channel between the earth and the sky.

While you continue breathing steadily – visualize the energy of your aura merging with the energy of the vortex – "See" and feel the energy flowing clockwise around you, from left to right as it travels in front of you.

After you have done this for a period of time which feels comfortable, invoke the energy with a spoken prayer such as this: **I invoke the power of this vortex to clear away energy blockages in my system, and I invoke the power of this vortex to awaken my psychic abilities.**

There is no need for me to give you advanced instructions for this meditation, *energy is information.* As you tune in to these cosmic energies you will receive guidance. Your "inner voice" will tell you what to do.

As you do this meditation many thoughts and images may enter your mind, perhaps even images from past lives. *Ride the waves*. Concentrate on sending your consciousness into the energy. After you have meditated for a while, and you feel "well tuned," it is then a good time to pray for help, guidance and spiritual healing.

The Torus is the most common form of energy field. Research done by the Institute of Heartmath with the Superconducting Quantum Interference Device

Was it Plato who said that a teacher teaches what they need to know? I have spent a lot of time contemplating the mysteries of the heart, and I am convinced that the heart is really the place where the god within resides.

Anahata, The Heart Chakra

I suggest meditating on feeling the reality of our Heart Chakras, by sending our awareness within our chests to find the tiny star in our heart that is the *eye of the vortex,* where the pure power of Infinite Love pours through. Projecting our thoughts into this place with the words "I Love God," creates an attunement with the highest forces of creation.

Anahata

In Sanskrit, the Heart Chakra is *Anahata*. I suggest chanting Anahata.

http://heartmath.com

35

BASIC PRINCIPLES FOR WORKING WITH EARTH ENERGY

Those who want to truly understand the vortex experience must spend time meditating and practicing "tuning in" to the energy. It is not surprising that many people visit vortices and report "feeling nothing." Merely visiting a vortex is not usually going to have any noticeable effect upon a person, other than helping them feel good.

Vortex energy is subtle. Those who want to truly understand the vortex experience must spend time meditating and practicing tuning in to the energy.

Beginners can learn how to tune in to vortex energy by first giving themselves the mental command to "become aware" of the energy. A mental command such as this invokes the *will*.

Will is perhaps the most potent power that each human possesses. Every action that we undertake begins as an act of *will*. Don Juan called *will*, "Intent." I think that Intent is the same power that we call love, as love is the absolute power in the universe that creates and sustains all things. One of the differences in the way most people might interpret love, and how the Toltecs of Don Juan's lineage interpret Intent, is that Intent is not very sentimental.

Many of Don Juan's teachings were designed to help Carlos understand that spirit is directed by Intent, but not by logic, therefore, it is impossible to fully understand either spirit or Intent. Most schools of mysticism say that we should follow our hearts and allow spirit to manifest for us without our thoughts getting in the way. I agree.

BEGINNER'S VORTEX MEDITATION

Spend a few minutes relaxing, then practice taking proper breaths. After you have relaxed, quiet your mind, and then give yourself the mental command to sense the energy, or to merge with the energy of the vortex.

Even though you may think that you do not know how to do this, I can assure you that every person knows how to work with spirit. This knowledge comes to us from the intuitive level, the place of silent knowledge: the I AM.

When the mind has become quiet you should begin to sense the energy of the vortex. As you start to merge with the energy you may find that your meditation seems deeper or stronger than usual. You may also find that it becomes easy to enter an altered state of consciousness, or that you may begin to have the sensation that the energy around you is pulsing, or moving in waves. You may also be able to sense Earth Energy by holding your hands out in front of you, parallel with the ground. This may give the sensation of "energy."

A simple invocation such as this can be used to awaken yourself to the energy of a vortex or power spot:

I Open Myself To Receive The Blessings Of The Infinite Spirit In All Things.

*The ancient mystics from whom we have inherited so much metaphysical wis -
dom understood that all things are energy, and that every form of energy has a
frequency, a vibrational rate. These early philosophers referred to all vibration
as sound. Traditionally, schools of yoga and mystic wisdom have taught that
the universe itself produces an endless sound, which we call "OM."*

Those who are on the spiritual path find that chanting simple syllables such as
OM helps them integrate their personal energy fields with the universe.

Chanting in a power spot can amplify the power of our chant. Even those who
have little experience in these matters find that ceremonial chanting at a power
spot can expand their consciousness considerably. A short chanting session can
have a very noticeable effect upon one's state of mind. Chanting opens up our psy -
chic centers and balances our energy patterns.

In Sedona, we like to go to the places of the rocks and chant OM. This sort of
chanting serves to "wake up" and balance the energies of the earth, as well as the
energies of those doing the chanting.

Earth healing ceremonies such as the medicine wheel should have a chanting
session before or after the opening prayer. This helps to bring the group's energy
into harmony.

To feel the power of the sound OM, one needs only to chant it correctly for a
while. Intoning the OM is an art: if you are not taught how to do it properly, it is
hard to understand exactly how it is done. When you chant OM, it is not really as if
you are saying OM at all. The sound is OOOOOOOOOOOOMMMMMMMM.
The muscles of the solar plexus should be used to project a resonant sound
throughout your space.

By properly chanting OM, the whole body is made to resonate harmoniously.
Therefore our energy becomes balanced, and we are able to open up to the higher
forms of psychic energy that are available.

Most Americans will feel a little silly when they first start doing this chant;
that is ok. Chanting is not a basic part of our culture, yet....

If you came upon a group of people who were trying to chant OM, but doing it
incorrectly, you would think that they looked a little silly. If you came up on these
same people a little while later, and they were chanting OM correctly, you might
wonder what planet they came from....

Chanting OM helps us to tune into the energy of the earth. We know that
electromagnetic waves of Earth Energy occur at frequencies (vibrations) just be -
low the range of human hearing; therefore, when we chant OM we may find reso -
nance with harmonic overtones of the earth Wave.

 - OM

Boynton Canyon is considered by many to be the most sacred and magical place in the Red Rock Country. When I gaze at the red rocks I sometimes feel as if the canyon were the landscape of dreams.

There is a "mysterious presence" in this Canyon which cannot be properly described with words. Many visitors experience what yogis and mystics refer to as deja vu: The feeling that one has been to this place before....

When gazing at the rocks, one often feels as if the enchanted landscape is almost within reach. Experiences of the waking world seem to merge with the reflections of the shadow world, and the spirits of the Indians who lived here before seem to be active and beckoning us to follow them into infinity.

It is difficult for me to convey my feelings about what I think is happening in Boynton Canyon without sounding too far-out, particularly in regard to what I think this electromagnetic vortex *might* be. Suffice it to say that our waking world probably does exist side by side with mysterious parallel realities. and that Boynton Canyon is a classic shamanic "crack" between these worlds. and that some of the ancient native people who lived in this canyon may well have been powerful Shaman's who achieved a type of immortality.

Over the years I have seen a number of photographs taken at the small spire just below Kachina Woman formation and at an Indian ruin near the back gate of the resort, that have an unusual blue aura in them. This aura is seen either hanging in the air, or around people. Many people feel that this blue light is the energy of a spirit, but it could also be a form of life force energy known as "orgone."

A number of psychics and channels have claimed that aliens use this vortex. I do not believe everything that has been channeled about this canyon, particularly about there being a secret base *below* the resort. But it does seem that non-physical entities do conduct some type of business in the canyon, as on one occasion while I was meditating deep in the canyon in the middle of the night during the summer solstice, I had the distinct impression that some type of alien or angelic beings came to me and gave me what they called a *"neurogenetic reprogramming."*

I have been able to sense the spiritual forces of the earth since I was a child. They are very dynamic, but also very subtle and tend to affect the body (in the chest area) more than they affect the mind. When I visit Boynton Canyon I frequently experience these energies as a feeling of *power* and mystery in my body, accompanied by a small perceptual shift that makes everything seem to subtly *shimmer.* This effect is comparable to viewing a mirage in the desert.

When we encounter a mirage we usually have the impression we are viewing a body of water such as a lake, but this image is only an illusion hanging in the air. The mirage has partially covered the landscape with a non-physical image made purely of waves of light. This is what I sometimes see in Boynton Canyon, *a subtle distortion of the landscape as if the air were moving in visible waves.*

Boynton Canyon can be a wonderful place for initiation into the mysteries of the earth. I suggest that you spend time there praying, meditating and setting your intention on contacting the spirit of the canyon. If your prayers come from the heart and are not ego-directed, you may experience an initiation/activation that will awaken your psychic abilities and strengthen your spirit bond with the earth.

This activation may be extremely subtle, occurring on the inner planes; but if you continue to build your power and study, you may look back on your visit to Boynton Canyon and see that you were in a truly magical, enchanted place. That you did contact spirit, and that your prayers had a definite life-changing effect.

If you are serious about exploring the mysteries of Boynton Canyon, it is a good idea to find yourself a personal power spot where you can settle in and do some serious meditating, a place that you can return to time and time again, physically and spiritually. One of the best places for this is the Kachina Woman formation at the mouth of the canyon near the parking lot. You need go no further to experience the spirit of the canyon.

Simply stated, those who wish to contact the spirit of the earth should enter a state of meditation with their Intent (*will*) focused on that task.

Do you think that the spot you have chosen has an energy that affects your mind? and if it does, does this energy agree with you? If the spot you have chosen doesn't feel right after you have been there awhile, or if you suddenly find yourself thinking negative thoughts, try another spot.

⊕   ⊕   ⊕

One of the easiest places to experience electrical Earth Energy in Boynton Canyon is a rock spire near the mouth of the canyon, which locals have named the Kachina Woman.

Since the effects of electrical vortices are often much more pronounced than magnetic vortices, the Kachina Woman has become a place that many people think of as *the* power spot in Boyton Canyon. Those who visit the Kachina Woman will know that they have found a truly magical space.

The area around the Kachina Woman is an ideal place to offer prayers to the Great Spirit and the spirit of the earth. Using the energies that are present here, you should be able to raise your vibration and activate your mind in a way that allows you to tune into the more subtle magnetic energies that are present in this canyon.

During regular meditations our energy field often expands, and this can be a good thing. But you should remember that if you do not call your energy back and ground yourself, you will lose power. So when you have finished meditating, remember to give yourself a mental command to call all your energy back into its normal position around your body. At this time it is also helpful to focus your attention on your earth connection, allowing yourself to become well grounded.

39

There is a resort and several private homes in Boynton Canyon. Over the years many people have lamented that this somehow spoils the area. I do not agree; I feel that this is only a matter of perception. I find the energy around Sedona to be quite active and that most (not all) development in Sedona does not actually affect the energy as badly as some might imagine.

It is natural for people who are ecologically minded, or who believe the earth is aware, to recoil from all destruction of nature, and certainly from the development of such an apparently sacred place. Unfortunately, our society has taught us to get caught up in judgmental behavior that blinds us to the higher nature of things. Those who are truly interested in exploring mystical realities, or any sort of self-improvement, will of course avoid limiting themselves or others with judgments. Let us all hope that love is the highest power and that the brilliance of God's creation will always shine through in all things.

I have heard a lot of people complain about the resort, perhaps even going as far as to say that it is haunted or cursed. The canyon may well host a number of non-physical entities, but I do not think this causes any serious problems. As for curses, I feel that anytime one speaks badly or thinks negative thoughts about a person or a thing, they are sending energy that has the qualities of a curse. This resort must certainly have had a lot of negative energy directed toward it, but I assure the reader that things are going well out there, and it is an inspiring place to stay or have dinner. (Reservations are required. and no, I did not accept money or favors in return for a plug.)

Over the years I have heard a number of people complain that the tennis courts were "constructed over an Indian burial ground." I know of no one who is actually able to prove this, but I have decided that if it is true, it might not be as bad as some folks might think. After all, when one is dead and their body has returned to the earth, does it really make any difference if something is built on their grave? Some would say yes, others no, I say *perhaps*. But after years of musing over these things, I began to have fantasies of Indian spirits hanging out at the lounge, listening to the jazz band and wishing they could have a cold beer.

I have seen a lot of things that people who are relatively new to Arizona may not have seen. When I was a young boy traveling in southern Arizona, I remember seeing "sky burials" that consisted of platforms built of small trees.

I suspect that the ancient dwellers of Boynton Canyon may well have practiced sky burial, and if they did they may well have chosen the mountaintops for their final resting place, not the center of the canyon. But whatever the truth of this may be, let us pray that their souls are resting well.

I feel that the mind-altering atmosphere of Boynton Canyon is created by earth's electromagnetic life force as it cascades like water over the edge of the canyon. This creates vortices, and these vortices are windows to Infinity.

As I state in my **General Theory of the Sedona Vortex Phenomenon,** the earth's natural energies are made particularly active in Sedona because Sedona is at the leading edge of a monumental wave pattern in the earth's crust known as the Colorado Plateau. Put simply, there is a disturbance here in the earth's energy field. It is not negative, but it does cause the energies of the earth to become active and form vortices around the rock formations.

Over the years I have seen a number of photographs taken at the small spire just below Kachina Woman formation, and at an Indian ruin near the back gate of the resort that have an unusual blue aura in them. This aura is seen either hanging in the air, or around people.

Many people feel that this blue light is the energy of a spirit, but it could also be a form of life force energy known as *orgone*.

This spire is on the ridge, just below the Kachina Woman formation. It is close to the parking lot. To get here, resist the urge to hike straight toward this formation, instead find the trail around the base that goes to the side *opposite* the parking lot.

In Kirlian photography, an electrical charge is used to produce an aura that appears on film. In the case of the blue aura seen around the Kachina Woman, I feel that it is quite possible that the natural geo-electric current flowing through the rocks may create a charge in the air that allows our cameras to pick up the blue light of *orgone energy*, which was originally discovered by Willhelm Reich.

Science tells us that electrons are released by rock formations such as the ones we see in Sedona. These negative ions are energizing. I also think that there is an aspect to electricity that we do not understand, but has been known to exist since the most ancient times. and this life force energy flows along features of the landscape such as waterways and ridge lines. So that when we climb mountains we experience a natural high, especially at the summit.

Boynton Canyon is a box canyon. Unless one is willing to climb there is only one way in and one way out. The main trail goes for about three miles.

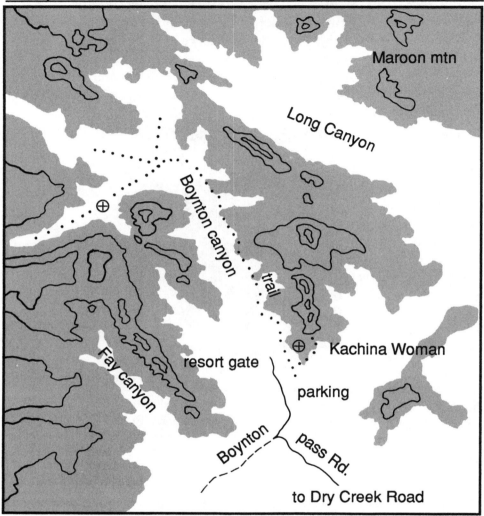

Hiking can be a distraction that keeps the consciousness fixed upon the physical world. It is only within the stillness of the quiet mind that one is able to experience the mysteries that lay beyond the veil....

ESTABLISH A MAGICAL SPACE
FOR POWER AND PROTECTION

Many people do not realize that the world of spirit holds dangers as well as rewards. Those who do not take precautions may open themselves to psychic attack.

Any time that you do any sort of meditation or other metaphysical work anywhere, it is a very good idea to pray to your guides and masters, asking them to protect you. It is also a good idea to establish a magical space as you meditate by visualizing a protective white or golden light surrounding yourself.

Whenever we meditate it is also helpful to consciously establish a "magical space" which we may think of as a private temple. Establishing and entering a magical space separates us from the ordinary world; *when we are in the temple we are meditating, praying and performing ceremonies.* The magic circle can also be used to protect those who are within the circle from undesirable outside influences.

The basic exercise for establishing a magical space is to claim the space you are in, and to visualize protective white or golden light coming into your aura from just above your head, filling the space around you. This actually feeds the aura and can make one stronger, and can be combined with the pillar of light meditation.

Many people who are seriously interested in working with the power of spirit use physical objects to establish their magical space. Circles can be scribed into soft soil or drawn with corn meal, or an elaborate layouts of crystals, stones, etc.

At some point you might like to get creative and build a circle of stones like a medicine wheel, but if you build one on public property I advise you to take your circle apart after the ceremony. If you do not unmake your circle, someone may come into your circle after you are gone and be affected by your energy, or affect you with their energy. This is not usually desirable.

Whether you are meditating at home or on the land, after you are done it is always a good idea to use the power of your *will* to call all of your energies back into their normal position, using your earth connection to ground yourself.

Mystic traditions vary, but we do know that the circle is the most basic form which we can use to mark the boundaries of the magical space. The two most significant variations of the basic circular form are the six-pointed "Star of David," and the five-pointed Pentagram. (Why is the military center of the U.S. a five-sided building?)

The Airport Vortex is the most accessible vortex in the Sedona area. It is an electric vortex, and its energy is some of the most easily felt, but you must re - member that this "electricity" does not strike like a thunderbolt; it is a subtle force which affects the mind and body from within.

Many people who visit this vortex, whether they are metaphysically oriented or not, will agree that they can sense the "electricity in the air." This is another way of saying that one feels good, and full of life. Feeling good is the body's reaction to electrical vortex energy.

Since it is so easy to experience the energy of the Airport Vortex, it is an excel - lent place for beginners to go in order for them to "get the feel." As one works with this vortex, the body's energy level will increase. This will energize both the *central nervous system* and the subtle energy system in much the same way that yoga exercises are known to do, thus allowing one to experience the altered states of consciousness that are associated with psychic phenomenon.

Working with the energies of the Airport Vortex, or any of the other power spots around Sedona, can be a catalyst that helps awaken psychic abilities. This does not mean that we have to depend upon the energies of a vortex to find the proper atmosphere for meditation. Once we have had our initiation at a vortex we should be able to begin to fly on our own.

The vortex occurs in the area of the two small hills. The energy field is bipolar, and is divided into two "lobes" around the hills. I think the energy travels up the gorge that divides these hills. From the area of the cliff that runs along the base of the hills you may get the impression that the vortex itself is actually hanging in midair, just beyond the cliff, above the gorge.

The area between the two small hills is considered by many to be as close to the "eye of the vortex" as a person can get without actually being able to float in midair above the gorge....

Perhaps the best place to encounter the energy of this vortex is at the summit of either of the two small hills. Electrical Earth Energy tends to travel up through the earth until it reaches the summit of a mountain, hill or other formation (such as a spire). It is then discharged into the air. By tuning in to the energy being emitted from these hills we find harmony with the spirit of the earth.

The easiest trail to the quiet inner part of the vortex area runs along the top of the cliff, between these two hills. If you encounter a medicine wheel somewhere along the ledge that forms the cliff that this trail travels over, you have found a good place to offer a traditional gift of tobacco or corn to the earth.

The energy of the Airport Vortex is ideally suited for awakening our psychic abilities; one of the most effective meditations for taking advantage of the energies at this vortex is the sunset meditation. (See page 46)

THE AIRPORT VORTEX

To reach Airport Vortex take Airport Road, off Highway 89. The parking lot is a little way past the last house on the left, about half way up Airport Hill.

The two hills of Airport Vortex are separated by a steep gorge. Both of these hills are wonderful places to experience vortex energy, but I think that the main part of the vortex is actually in the air between the hills.

One of my favorite places is a terrace at the edge of the gorge between the two hills. The trail is very easy to find; it begins at the parking lot and follows the fence heading north. It only takes a few minutes to walk up this trail and it is much safer than attempting to climb either hill.

Please note that the two hills of the Airport Vortex are so small they do not show up on this map.

The picture above was taken from the east side looking west. The parking lot is on the other side, and most people do not see this view.

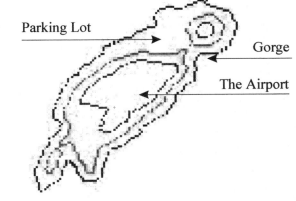

Parking Lot

Gorge

The Airport

The summits of either of the two hills at the Airport Vortex are particularly good places to watch the sunset.

The sunset meditation is a very simple, yet powerful technique. As you gain power by doing this meditation, your psychic abilities will become awakened. This meditation should give you an immediate energy boost and a heightened state of consciousness which can help you "go within" to meditate and pray.

The key to this meditation is to gaze towards the west and concentrate upon absorbing the colors of the sunset. **(Never look directly at the sun itself.)**

Get to the place where you are planning to meditate well before the sun actually sets, allowing yourself plenty of time to calm down before you actually begin to meditate.

Once the sun has touched the horizon, it takes a little less than five minutes for it to disappear. This gives us a definite time span for this meditation: Everyone should be able to hold their attention for five minutes.

You may either sit or stand to do this meditation. Be sure to focus part of your consciousness on your connection with the earth; this will complete the energy circuit between the sun and the earth, thus lowering your resistance to the high energy light communication that you are preparing yourself to receive.

SUNSET MEDITATION

1.   Feel your connection with the earth.

2.   Breathe through your nose, using the muscles of your abdomen to draw in your breath.

3.   As you watch the sunset, give yourself a mental command to "absorb" light energy through your eyes.

4.   Every time you take a breath, visualize yourself absorbing light energy. "See" this light energy flowing through your body, from your third eye to your solar plexus.

5.   As you breathe in, visualize the light energy going into your forehead as it is drawn into your belly. When you exhale, visualize the energy flowing through your body and out of your forehead.

6.   Close your eyes and concentrate on your third eye, "seeing" and feeling light energy from the sun entering your system through your third eye. Keep breathing; keep the energy circulating.

7.   Alternately open your eyes, drinking in the light with your eyes and with your breath. Then close your eyes and "see" the light of the sun with your third eye.

8.   **Do not look directly at the sun**; gaze toward the west.

46

ESTABLISHING YOUR ENERGY BOND WITH THE EARTH:
WE ARE THE RAINBOW BRIDGE

As you do sunset meditations or any other meditations it is important to estab - lish your bond with the earth. This completes our body's natural energy circuit with the planet.

Every human being has a natural energy connection with the earth. Our pri- mary contact points with the earth are the soles of our feet and the base of our spi - nal column. If we want to explore the world of spirit, it is very important to strengthen these connections with the earth. Without good earth contact, people become ungrounded, "floaty," and unable to control their energies.

When you want to work with Earth Energy you should use the power of your *will* to consciously reinforce your "earth connection." Do this by visualizing "roots" coming out from the bottoms of your feet and the base of your spine, "see" these roots with your mind's eye, going deep into the earth, connecting you firmly to the mother. Use your power of creative visualization to "see" energy traveling up from the earth into your feet and the base of your spine. This exercise helps you to establish a firm earth connection.

Another powerful form of this meditation is to draw energy into the earth. This connection completes the circuit between our father sun and our mother earth, making the person who completes this circuit a "Rainbow Bridge." This type of meditation energizes and balances the energy of the meditator.

For serious meditation on the energy of the earth, the feet should be bare. This enhances your contact with the earth, and helps subtle energies of spirit flow through your system in the manner nature intended. The classic position for working with Earth Energy is standing. The body becoming a "grounding rod."

Another excellent way to strengthen your energy bond with the earth is to put as much of your body as possible in contact with the earth. This exercise will balance your energy, and it can be done before or after any other meditation.

Lie face down upon the soil, the sand, or a rock and feel yourself merging with the earth. Invoke the power of your *will* with the mental command to *merge with the energy of the earth*, and allow yourself to feel that the energy centers at your third eye and solar plexus are sending out "feelers" into the earth that bring healing and relaxing energy into your body. One can also do this meditation laying on their back; in this case, I suggest concentrating on bringing energy into your kidneys.

⊕　⊕　⊕

CATHEDRAL ROCK MAP

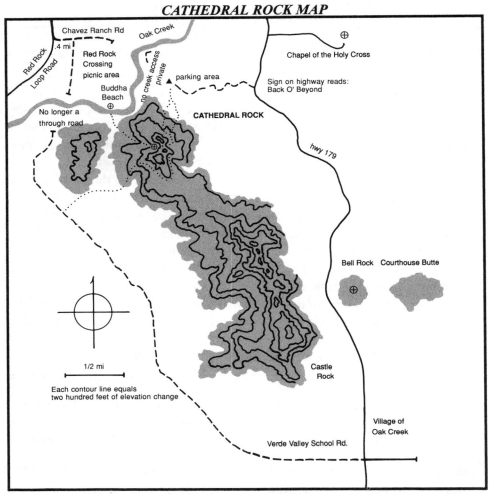

Each contour line equals two hundred feet of elevation change. Paved roads are marked with solid lines, dirt roads with dashed lines, trails with dots.

Most people can easily feel the current of Earth Energy that flows with the waters that pass by the foot of this formation, but will never have the chance to hike to the "saddle" between the towers. If you do decide to climb to the saddle, I suggest that you do not head up from the creek side, as this route is far more difficult that the eastern route that starts at "Back O' Beyond."

Please do not attempt to climb Cathedral Rock, or any other of the sandstone formations in the Sedona area unless you are an experienced hiker with some experience climbing, or you are with someone who does have experience.

Remember that rock in the Sedona area tends to be crumbly. And rock on the sides of Cathedral Rock tends to flake off – the place you have decided to stand may come loose! So keep your eyes open, and your hands out of your pockets.

The image of Cathedral Rock's sandstone towers casting their reflection in the water is perhaps the ultimate statement of Sedona's visual magnificence.

Many people find the energies of Cathedral Rock to have a special quality that brings inner peace, a feeling of union with nature and a sense of the awesome power behind God's creation as it is reflected into the goddess of the earth.

As human beings, we have a natural attraction to beautiful places such as this and usually find them to be quite healing to the mind, body and (hopefully) the soul. Throughout history, our ancestors have identified places such as Cathedral Rock as having a unique healing quality, so it is not unusual that as western civilization moved westward we have discovered places such as this.

In Sedona, we have found a rather colorful word to describe these places, and indeed, this word is quite accurate. Cathedral Rock is a "magnetic vortex," and in support of this we find that there is a large deposit of iron-bearing basalt running through the center of the formation from east to west, and that basalt intrusions such as this have magnetic fields that are detectable by magnetometers.

The basalt intrusion and its relatively weak magnetic field are, however, probably *not* what produces the vortex. Instead, I would like to propose that the Cathedral Rock Vortex is the result of a complex wave pattern that is part of the geology of the Colorado Plateau, and that the unique structure of Cathedral Rock, its basalt intrusion and the vortex associated with them are the result of the same quantum forces that govern chaos theory and the fractal nature of reality.

Magnetism is an aspect of Kundalini, which is the basic primal life force of the universe. In human beings, Kundalini is noted for its energizing effects and is associated with sexuality (the power to create life). It is easy to feel the current of life force energy around the base of Cathedral Rock. All one needs to do is stand near the water as they face Cathedral Rock from the west and open their arms wide and breathe, or perhaps do some freestyle Tai Chi.

Most of this current of energy around the base of the formation does not come directly from Cathedral Rock itself. Instead, *it flows through the area with the waters of Oak Creek,* which, like all healthy waterways, is a natural generator and conductor of Earth Energy. When this current of energy comes into contact with the base of the formation it changes direction from south to west; this releases energy into the area.

I think that the vortex reacts with the Earth Energy that flows past it. This has an effect similar to an electric generator or motor and may actually fuel the vortex causing it to become stronger.

I have spent many hours and a number of nights around the bases of the rock spires of Cathedral Rock, and I am pretty sure that there really is an interdimensional window hovering about, somewhere above the basalt intrusion. and it is quite likely that high-level beings such as angels use this vortex.

A magnet produces a field that draws the space around it into an ordered en-ergetic flow. Magnetic resonance with the earth's energy field is a desirable state that occurs naturally to all beings on the planet. Vortex explorers have found that the strong field of the Cathedral Rock Vortex can supply a boost that has very desirable effects.

At Cathedral Rock you are in an energy field that allows you to become very connected and in tune with the earth. Establishing a strong connection with the earth is very important to everyone's spiritual development. By tuning into this field of energy and resonating with it, you may experience a realignment of the energy field of your body, which can be very beneficial to your overall health and well-being, and your state of consciousness.

To draw the energy in, it is helpful to find a place on the formation that feels right for you. Once you have found a good spot, I suggest doing a little physical exercise to get your energy flowing. If you are not used to exercising or are em-barrassed to do so because people might be watching, simply meditate on the experience of just being there. Then use the power of your *will* to tune in to the vortex, giving yourself the mental command to absorb energy.

Cathedral Rock is also an excellent place for sunset meditations. These med-itations are described both in the Airport Vortex section and in the section on Color Meditations. If you meditate on the sun at Cathedral Rock, I am certain that you will experience a powerful altered state of consciousness. I suggest you take advantage of every opportunity to absorb the sacred energy of the sun.

CRYSTAL DREAM CAVERN MEDITATION:
A DREAM FANTASY MEDITATION

It is helpful to pray to your guides and masters for guidance and protection before you do this meditation.

This dream fantasy can be done at a vortex, or at home. You can have a friend read this meditation to you as you relax, or you can read it to yourself and use the ideas in this meditation to guide you in creating your own journey.

Relax, feel yourself merging with the waves of magnetic energy that are emanating from the rocks. Use the power of your Will to consciously tune in to the vortex energy. Do this by giving yourself the mental command to "merge with the energy." Breathe deep, relaxed breaths.

You can feel that there is a source of radiant energy pulsing with power deep in the rocks below you. It is as if there were a tiny sun within the rocks emanating warm, inviting waves of energy.

Go within your mind and see yourself as if you were in a dream. Since you are now in the dreamtime and no longer limited to the rules of the waking world, simply Will yourself to move toward this warm radiant source of healing Earth Energy that is sending its vibrations through the rocks.

Feel yourself passing through the rocks, their substance gently massaging your spirit as you move through them. As you project yourself toward the mysterious power source within the earth you suddenly find yourself transported to the heart of the crystal cave.

The crystals of this cavern glow with a warm healing golden light, and you feel as if you were in an pleasant warm ocean of sparkling electrical energy. You are drawn to a crystal which fits comfortably in your hand. As you pick it up, a telepathic "voice" tells you that you are about to partake in the direct experience of God's divine radiant love.

The crystal begins to produce warm pulses of electrical energy which fill your being with pure ecstatic joy. As this happens your energy centers open up and you become a channel of pure rainbow light energy as God's divine sevenfold beam of brightness and illumination awakens your energy centers.

As you become filled with this healing energy the entire cavern begins to glow with one particular color, which is it? Red? Turquoise? Violet? or maybe Blue, Yellow, or Orange? Whatever color it is, this is either the color of your power, or your healing.

Suddenly you find yourself back in your physical body. Lie there for a moment remembering your crystal journey, then give yourself the mental command to "become fully present in your body." Sense that all parts of your consciousness have returned to their normal waking positions. Open your eyes; awaken to the dream.

The Chapel is a great monument to the power of the Christ.

The Chapel of the Holy Cross receives more visitors than any other power spot in Sedona. It has been a place of spiritual healing and guidance for many people who would never think of visiting a vortex. The cross represents interweaving of forces that unite to form the physical universe. It is the union of the male and the female energies – LOVE.

The Chapel of the Holy Cross is in the same valley as Cathedral Rock and Bell Rock. Sunsets seen from the Chapel offer an inspiring view of Cathedral Rock..

Over the years the certain members of the Sedona Christian community have ridiculed New Agers, saying that we "worshiped rocks." Many of these people were probably unaware that the center of the Christian, Hebrew and Muslim faiths is a large rock in the Temple of the Dome of the Rock in Jerusalem.

Since time immemorial humans have found that, for whatever reason, some rocks and rock formations have a spiritual quality. One of the best examples of this is the stone that the Old Testament prophet Joseph, laid his head on when he had his vision of the ladder that lead to heaven. This stone is highly prized and is said to rest under the coronation throne in Westminster Abby.

I do not think that anyone has spent much time actually worshiping the rocks in Sedona, but most people find it easy to sense that Sedona d

oes have a special aura that places it in the same category as some of the great shrines of mystery and healing that were venerated by our ancestors.

FIRE AND WATER
THE SAN FRANCISCO PEAKS AND MONTEZUMA'S WELL

These two places of power represent two rather distinct and seemingly opposite aspects of Earth Energy. To the north of Sedona stand the San Francisco Peaks: ancient volcanos, places of sometimes frightening creative power. To the south of Sedona we find Montezuma's Well, a place that invites all who visit to bask in the healing spirit of the earth mother.

The San Francisco Peaks are a dominant force in the spiritual beliefs of the Hopi, Navajo and Yavapai tribes. These tribes believe that powerful earth and sky spirits (Kachinas) inhabit the area of these peaks. They feel that these peaks are very sacred, and great care is taken not to insult the spirits of this place.

The highest of these four peaks is also the highest mountain in Arizona: Mount Humphreys (12,643 feet). It is interesting to note that the canyons of Sedona are carved into the feet of the mountains which are crowned by the San Francisco Peaks.

MONTEZUMA'S WELL

As children of the earth we are born into this world with a spiritual bond to the earth that draws us to enchanted oases such as Montezuma's Well. The legends of the human race refer to many places such as this – sacred wells. Places of healing, where the spirit of man is touched by the caress of the earth.

The legends of the Apache Indians speak of Sedona and the Verde Valley as the place where their tribe originated. Their legends say that the mother of all the Apache people emerged from the earth through Montezuma's Well, which is about 25 miles south of Bell Rock, and that she lived in **Boynton Canyon**. She is said to have become pregnant from the energy of the sun, and given birth to the original members of their tribe. To this day members of various tribes, including the Hopi, draw water out of Montezuma's Well and use it for ceremonial purposes.

Montezuma's Well is a natural feature of the landscape, created in much the same manner that the sinkholes of Sedona were formed: *by water flowing through the earth.* Geologists believe that this water created caverns that extend from the San Francisco Peaks to Montezuma's Well, and that the sinkholes of Sedona are entrances to these caverns. Unfortunately, the sinkholes are completely unsafe and the would-be entrances to the caverns are full of rubble.

SCHNEBLY HILL AND "THE MEDICINE WHEEL"

The Schnebly Hill formation stands alone at the mouth of Oak Creek Canyon, across from Wilson Mountain and Uptown Sedona.

The Schnebly Hill area is a place of power and spirit. So many people have come to recognize this area as a power spot that it has become common to hear it referred to as the Schnebly Hill Vortex. During the time of the Harmonic Convergence many people gathered on a large flat formation in the middle of Bear Wallow canyon and constructed a large medicine wheel that was approximately 150 feet across. For several years this medicine wheel had been the focal point for many earth healing ceremonies, and many people who have traveled to Sedona remember their visits to this wheel as one of the most magical, spiritual and healing experiences of their lives.

I led full moon, solstice and equinox ceremonies there for about two years, around 1990 and 1992, but finally got tired of the rough road and began to work closer to town. After a while another group started doing "ceremonies" up there that were primarily just a bunch of wild folks banging on drums. I went to a few of these events and realized that it was causing a disturbance in the energetics of the area. I tried to tell these folks that they were causing problems with the energy grids of Sedona, but they just said I was on an ego trip.

Ultimately the Forest Service went up there and threw the rocks off the edge of the formation, leaving little material to rebuild the wheel. This is one of the few cases where I agree with what they did. There were a lot of strange things going on up there and it needed to come to an end, at least for a while. Many people have fond memories of this place, and perhaps someday we will gather there again.

Schnebly Hill Road goes all the way to the highlands and ultimately merges with Highway 17. Today it is a very rough road.

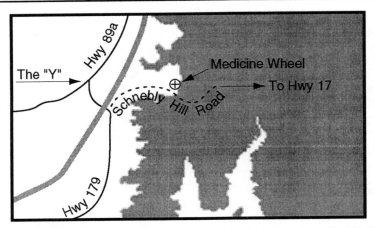

Sunset Point 1.5 Mi From "Y" – Medicine Wheel 3.8 mi from "Y."

Chapter 5

Meditations For Developing
Psychic Abilities

Color meditations serve to balance the energy of the body and awaken the body's en-ergy centers. These energy centers are known to us by the ancient Sanskrit word: CHAKRA.

The art and science of color meditation has been practiced for thousands of years by yogis and mystics. The ability to "work with light" is the most valuable skill a human being can master. As the Master Jesus said: "I Am The Light." All those who work with light are establishing a bridge between themselves and the highest spiritual beings in the universe. Not all forms of light can be seen with our physical eyes....

Color meditations will quickly open you up to the direct experience of metaphysical light energy (Prana). You will be working with light energy that comes directly from the sun; your mind and body will become energized and spiritually healed. "Light pro-grams" contained within the genetic code and nerve structure are activated...psychic awareness is increased.

The seven chakras of the human aura, and the energy channels that run parallel to the nerve channel of the spinal column, are often referred to as the "Rainbow Bridge." Each chakra is associated with a gland in the physical body. These glands are transfer points (transducers) between the non-physical realm of the light energies and the physical body. When a chakra is stimulated it causes a gland in the physical body to secrete hormones which are "trigger mechanisms" that alter the body's chemistry and lead to altered states of consciousness.

The higher chakras, which are located in the brain, are the energy centers which serve as our contact points to the higher realms of consciousness. When activated, these energy centers work with the pineal and the pituitary glands, which are our physical or-gans of "extrasensory perception," capable of sending and receiving signals of pure light energy.

Our "third eye" psychic center, the pineal gland, works with our "solar plexus" to absorb, circulate and control energy (otherwise known as light) throughout our body.

"Solar plexus" is a proper medical term: A plexus is a place where blood vessels or nerves come together and intertwine. The solar plexus is the center of the human body. Since ancient times it has been known to be our body's center of vitality and connection point with the solar mind. The solar plexus is located just below our rib cage in the cen-ter of our body. Proper breaths are drawn through the nose with the muscles of the abdo-men and the solar plexus. Breathing through the mouth dulls the mind.

Color meditations are always done with breathing exercises. Oxygen that has been charged by the sun is taken into the body with the breath. The action of the breath-ing muscles of the solar plexus circulates the light force energy through the body.

There are two basic forms of color meditation: Those which focus the meditator's mind upon specific colors, and those in which the meditator concen-trates upon becoming "aware of the light."

When we do color meditations and light meditations, we become Rainbow Warriors. Illumination occurs when we become filled with the light of the Great Spirit. As we become illuminated, our bodies become strengthened and healed. The true purpose of our life is revealed to us and we are able to contact our higher selves, our soul consciousness. By practicing these meditations we are learning to direct spiritual energy with the power of our *will*.

Generally, when we speak about color meditations we are talking about "open eye" meditations upon sources of colored light, or visualizations of specific colors. This is somewhat different from "becoming aware of the light."

When becoming aware of the light, consciousness is focused on pure spiritual energy as it is perceived by the third eye. The most potent forms of this spiritual light are perceived by mystics to be the White, Golden and Violet Rays.

Simply "meditating upon the light" is an excellent meditation for developing psychic awareness. With the eyes closed, one uses the power of creative visualiza-tion to "see" a white or golden light with the mind's eye.

This light enters our personal energy field from just above the head at the soul/body energy transfer point (the eighth chakra). Students of metaphysics know that this light is not imaginary; it is a very real spiritual force which human beings have the power to invoke.

Many students of metaphysics find that meditating upon specific visual colors can be a very powerful, energizing and energy-balancing meditation. The basic form of the visual color meditation is given in the Airport Vortex section.

Perhaps the most notable color meditation is the sunset meditation. Concen-trating upon the golden light of the sun energizes and balances the body's energy system.

Another powerful form of this meditation is to concentrate upon an intensely green light such as that given off by grass or trees in the full sunlight. Meditating upon the color green stimulates the heart chakra, balances the energy of the aura and heals the body.

A powerful color meditation involves focusing our mind's eye upon each chakra, one at a time, beginning with the root chakra, moving upward to the crown chakra.. As each chakra is concentrated upon, the color which is associated with that chakra is visualized flowing in and out of the chakra with the breath.

Each of the chakras has a *seed syllable* which can be chanted to activate that particular chakra. OM is the seed syllable for the 6th and 7th chakras. Chanting OM is one of the easiest ways to elevate the consciousness.

Various schools and teachers have different systems for interpreting the subtle energies that flow in the body and it is likely that not all humans are "wired" the same way, or respond to sounds in the same way.

I like to chant Aloha, and find that this sound does wonders for the awareness. I also like to chant Anahata, which is the Sanskrit name for the Heart Chakra, and Hum.

The Sanskrit Seed-Syllable Hum

Please note the flaming drop and the crescent moon at the apex of the Hum symbol, this illustrates the masculine creative power of the universe activating the feminine magnetic power of the universe.

I think that one of the most important things to be aware of is that we do not live in a universe of duality, we live in a universe of trinity. Love is the point of unity and balance.

The seven energy centers of yoga are vortices that are attuned to specific ener-
gies and vibrations. Each one of these "chakras" works in harmony with one
of the glands of the endocrine system.

⊕   The Crown Chakra works with the pineal gland, the master gland of the endocrine system. This gland contains light receptor cells similar to the eye and produces hormones that control the other glands. Meditation, yoga and diet help this
gland produce indoles that can trigger profound states of heightened awareness.

⊕   The Brow Chakra works with the pituitary gland. This chakra is often called
the "third eye," but anatomically and energetically the true third eye is the pituitary
gland.

⊕   The Throat Chakra is a powerful energy center. Its gland is the thyroid. The
Throat Chakra is associated with sound (vibration). In metaphysical terms, sound
is one of the primary energies of the universe. With our voices we "create" sound
energy. Sound moves matter.

⊕   The Heart Chakra is the center of our energy system. Its gland is the thymus.
The Heart Chakra helps balance the lower primal forms of life force energy with
the higher forms of light energy. It is also our connection to Infinity.

⊕   The Third Chakra, or solar plexus, is the body's center of life-giving vitality. It
works with the adrenal gland. It is known to mystics and yogis around the world as
the seat of the *will*. According to the system of the Native Americans, it is the center of our being. The solar plexus works with the third eye to draw light energy into
our system. When you do color meditations, focus on your breathing. As you
breathe, visualize light energy circulating through your third eye and your solar
plexus. Your solar plexus is known to radiate and absorb energy. This is described
quite nicely in Carlos Castaneda's *Tales of Power.* Strands of light fibers (Akashic
Threads), which exist on the etheric plane, radiate from our solar plexus and connect us to the world. Jose Argüelles refers to these fibers in *The Mayan Factor,* as
the umbilical cord of (*or to*) the universe. On one occasion I was jolted out of this
reality and saw thin filaments of light connecting people together.

⊕   The Second Chakra is said to reside in various places in the abdomen. In Tao-
ist practices it is usually thought to be the space of three fingers below the navel.
They believe this chakra to be our basic life force center and of great importance to
the general vitality of the organs in the lower body. Strength in this energy center is
necessary for controlling out-of-body experiences.

⊕   The Root Chakra is located at the base of the spine and the perineum. This
chakra is our connection with the mother earth and her primal life force energy.
The Root Chakra, the Second Chakra and the Third Chakra work together to help
the body harness the primal life force energy of the universe, *Kundalini.* Some of
the most potent forms of yoga group the three lower chakras together.

The third eye can be stimulated by applying "pressure" to it. This pressure is something that most people can learn to become aware of by concentrating within your head on the area above and between your eyes. Some yoga teachers would say to "gaze upward" with your eyes closed.

Your third eye is affected by breathing exercises. It works with your solar plexus to absorb and circulate energy through your energy system.

This meditation directly stimulates the Third Eye. Once the Third Eye is stimulated certain things begin to happen automatically. Listen to your inner voice. It will tell you what to do.

THIRD EYE MEDITATION

⊕ Relax while you sit up straight with both feet on the floor. Use your *will* to make your connection with the earth.

⊕ Take proper breaths through your nose, using the muscles of your abdomen and solar plexus to draw the air in - *relax..*

⊕ After you feel that your breathing has become steady, let all your breath out and hold it. While you are doing this, focus on your Third Eye and concentrate until you really must breathe. Then you may go ahead and breathe.

⊕ ⊕ ⊕

This exercise will stimulate the Third Eye.

You should feel a natural high after this exercise.

After you start to become conscious of your third eye, you may experience physical sensations in that area of the forehead. This is natural, and it is good .

Placing quartz crystals on the third eye is an
excellent way to awaken your psychic abilities.

THIRD EYE MEDITATION II

⊕ Sit up straight and make your "earth connection." Breathe properly, imagine that you are circulating energy with your breath.

⊕ Pay careful attention to the act of breathing. Notice the air going in, and out of your nose. Visualize the muscles of your solar plexus drawing energy into your body and circulating it throughout your system.

⊕ Think of the air as energy. Imagine that as you draw in each breath some of this energy is also being drawn into your third eye and energizing it. After you do this for awhile, exhale completely and concentrate on your third eye. Go deep inside and apply "pressure" to your third eye.

Meditations using spiraling energy have been used by students of metaphysics for thousands of years. There are many variations of the basic technique, including the pop-ular Merkaba meditation taught Drunvalo Melchizedek.

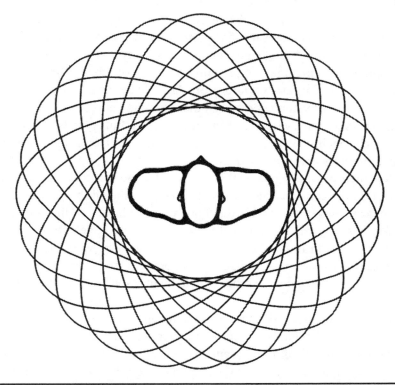

Energy moving in a clockwise direction into the earth is considered to be the most healing and energizing. This is the "way of the sun." To gather energy focus your Intent on moving the energy in this direction.

As with all meditations, it is important to relax for a while before you actually begin to do the meditation. Breathing properly is also very important; remember that a proper breath is drawn through the nose, and the muscles of the abdomen are used to draw the breath in. This meditation helps put us in touch with the natural energy flow of the earth. It is therefore important for the operator to establish a strong connection with the earth. This is done by giving yourself a mental command to "connect" with the earth, and by visualizing this happening.

Spiraling energy meditations are usually done standing up with the feet flat on the ground. You may stand with your legs either shoulder width apart, or together, depend-ing on how you feel at the time. The knees should be relaxed. That is to say, the leg should not be "locked," and the knees should be slightly bent.

Those who are interested in developing their psychic abilities can accelerate their learning by working with quartz crystals. Many people who take the time to learn how to use these crystals often find that knowledge comes to them directly from the "higher planes."

Quartz crystals, rubies, emeralds, sapphires etc. are formed within the earth by superheated water. Due to the volcanic activity in the Sedona area it is entirely possible that there may be deposits of various types of crystals deep within the faults that form the canyons of the red rock country. The mysterious energies we encounter throughout this area may be partially the result of energy fields produced by crystals. Whatever the case, we know for a fact that Sedona's sandstone formations contain countless tiny quartz crystals, otherwise known as sand...

Many crystals have valuable electronic qualities, but crystals of silicon dioxide (quartz) are probably the most electronically active. Silicon is the main ingredient of most transistors and integrated circuits.

While there are many people that may scoff at the idea that crystals could have any effect on the consciousness, it should be remembered that since the most ancient times mystics of all schools that I am aware of have said they do. This is one of the reasons why royalty adorned their crowns with jewels: to help channel in higher vibrations. In India, the prescription of precious jewels has been practiced for thousands of years. East Indian astrologers will frequently suggest that there clients obtain specific gems in order to help them resonate properly with planetary influences.

My own experience indicates that opening up to the energies of quartz crystals activates "circuitry" within our central nervous system that helps us become more aware of the energy field of our planet. However, merely wearing a quartz crystal will not always have a noticeable affect upon the consciousness. A crystal has to be worked with in order for it to become "activated."

Wearing a quartz crystal helps to develop an energy bond between the crystal, the person who is wearing it, and the earth. But in order for the wearer to actually work the crystal, it should be held in the hands during meditation, or it should be gazed at. Mental commands should be directed towards the crystal, asking it to wake up and do its work. A crystal can be asked to perform a function, such as protection, or it can be "listened to" for guidance.

Perhaps the quickest way to learn how to work with a crystal is to place it in the center of your forehead and then focus upon that spot. When you first begin to do this, do it for only a short while or else you might overload your circuitry.

CREATING A SACRED SPACE WITH INTENTION

We can make any space a sacred space with our intention. All schools of mysticism I am familiar with recommend calling in the light to bless and clear our homes and bodies of negative energies and entities.

Working with energy fields such as the pillar of light is an important aspect of ascension yoga. We create energy fields around ourselves to protect, heal and energize our bodies, our temples and our homes. The creation of energy fields is one of the first exercises students of yoga and mysticism learn. The body of light is activated and strengthened as you develop your ability to work with energy fields.

One of the most important concepts of ceremony and temple work is to claim the space by filling it with your presence, and then demanding out loud, in the name of the Lord God Creator of the universe that any and all negative entities that may be present leave and never return. As this is done, cleanse and purify the area by mentally creating a pillar of light that brings the universal love vibrations directly into your space and ask out loud that this be done.

Our bodies, our homes and our cars should also be blessed and purified in the manner described above. Blessing and exorcism are very important aspects of magic and shamanism. It is wise to use exorcism to make sure that no strange entities are lurking around your home, your temple, your associates, or yourself. **To avoid karmic penalties you must always ask permission to do any type of energy work or exorcism on anyone other than yourself.**

You will quite likely note a definite shift in energy around yourself and your home after you begin your blessings and exorcisms.

INVOCATION FOR EXORCISM OF NEGATIVE ENTITIES

I INVOKE THE HOLY SPIRIT

IN THE NAME OF THE LORD GOD CREATOR OF THE UNIVERSE.

I DEMAND THAT ANY and ALL NEGATIVE ENTITIES

WHO MAY BE ATTACHED TO ME ON THE INNER PLANES

OR THAT ARE OTHERWISE ATTEMPTING TO

MANIPULATE ME IN ANY WAY

LEAVE ME NOW!

I CALL OUT TO MY HIGHER SELF

I CALL OUT TO MY SOUL

I CALL OUT TO MY ANGELIC GUIDES,

BE WITH ME! GUIDE ME! PROTECT ME!

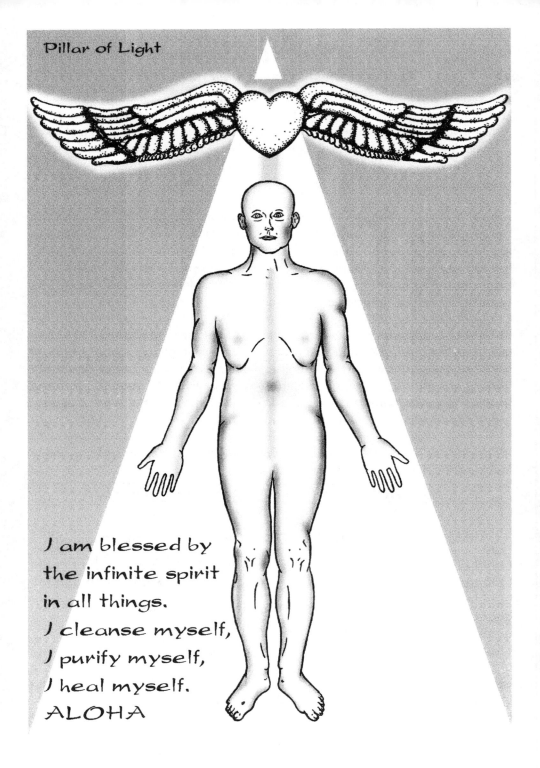

Pillar of Light

I am blessed by
the infinite spirit
in all things.
I cleanse myself,
I purify myself,
I heal myself.
ALOHA

THE PILLAR OF LIGHT – RAINBOW BRIDGE TO THE HIGHER SELF

The pillar of light and its central channel, the Antahkarana, are a two-way energy circuit, from the earth to the eighth chakra soul star, and from the eighth chakra back to the earth. To perform energy transformation of the physical body and to reprogram DNA, we must use the breath, visualization and the pillar of light/Antahkarana to draw Kundalini life force energy up from the earth and solar life force energy (Prana) down from the eighth chakra.

Earth Energy flows naturally into the chakras in the base of our feet and through the area around the tip of the spine and the perineum. It is good to meditate directly on the land, using the chakras at the tip of your spine, perineum and bottoms of your feet to send energetic roots deep into the earth.

Grounding ourselves into the earth is an important part of the ceremony of the pillar of light. *The Keys of Enoch* tells us that we must learn to heal the earth by invoking universal love as the Holy Spirit and projecting it into the earth. One of the ways to do this is to visualize yourself as part of an energy channel that extends to the very center of the earth, and then use your *will* to send love into our planet's heart.

THE PILLAR OF LIGHT AS A CHANNEL FOR UNIVERSAL LOVE

The Keys of Enoch mentions the pillar of light many times, making it clear that this is one of the most powerful transformational and protective techniques we can use.

⊕ The pillar of light is an important basic exercise.

⊕ Its practice can be traced back at least as far as the ancient Egyptians.

⊕ When using the pillar of light, the student makes a direct connection with their higher self/soul.

⊕ The pillar of light brings the student guidance from the entities who support the positive evolution of humanity.

⊕ The pillar of light energizes the student and brings the student's energy body into harmony.

⊕ The pillar of light forms a protective shield around the student.

⊕ The pillar of light can be used to cleanse the aura of negativity and blockages.

⊕ The pillar of light should be invoked before meditating or before doing healing work.

⊕ The pillar of light should be used in conjunction with the various invocations and prayers given in this book.

Stand with your feet spread about as far apart as the width of your head. Keep your knees slightly bent, as this allows energy to flow freely through the legs. If the knees are locked, the muscle tension will block the energy flow. After you have found your point of balance, visualize a pillar of gold or white light surrounding your body. See this pillar of light rising far above you and descending far below you into the earth.

Use your powers of creative visualization and *will* to draw soul star energy in through your crown chakra with your breath, then use your *will* to circulate this energy throughout your body.

See Spirit, Feel Spirit, Breathe Spirit.

Use the invocations that are given in this book to program the energies of the pillar of light to cleanse, purify and heal your body and mind.

I invoke my soul.
Be with me,
Shield me, protect me.
Help me learn how to create the pillar of light.
Aloha

⊕

I Am Universal Harmony.
I Am Universal Balance.
I Am Universal Love.
I Am Universal Life.
I Am Universal Light.
I Am One with the Infinite Universe.
I Am All Powerful.
I invoke the Power of Mental Clarity.

EARTH HEALING and PILLAR OF LIGHT EXERCISES

⊕ Use the pillar of light to send healing energy into the earth.

⊕ Use the pillar of light to send healing love into the earth.

⊕ Use the pillar of light to send prayers into the earth.

⊕ Use the pillar of light to send your consciousness into the earth.

The goal of all these exercises is to attune the physical body to the energies of the soul, thus allowing the energies of universal consciousness to merge with the conscious mind and physical body. This process occurs in stages and is governed by the student's willingness to do the work required to bring this into fruition.

I Am that I Am,
I call out to my soul, hear me:
Open the channel between us,
Activate the pillar of light,
cleanse this unit,
purify this unit,
heal this unit,
I open myself to receive
The blessings of the infinite spirit
In all things.

⊕

I ask the Holy Spirit to place a pillar of its Divine Essence over me.
I ask the Great Spirit for help, guidance and protection.
I invoke the presence of my soul.
Be with me, help me, guide me, protect me.
Show me the path to ascension
and everlasting life in ever-expanding life systems.

⊕

I Am that I Am,
I cancel, nullify and dissolve any and all
negative and undesirable energies or karma
I may have accumulated in this lifetime
Or any other lifetime
and I now activate and accept
the Christ Consciousness program
within every cell of my being.

INVOCATION OF THE SOUL FOR EXORCISM

I invoke the presence of my soul.
I *will* my soul to remove all entities
that may be attached to any of my bodies.
I *will* my soul to cancel, nullify and dissolve
any and all curses and hexes
that have ever been directed toward me,
or affected me in any way.

Antahkarana

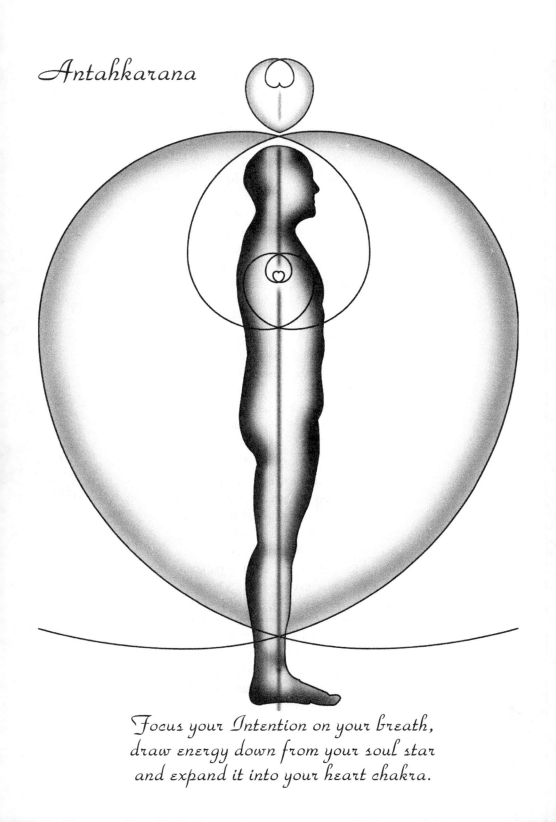

Focus your Intention on your breath, draw energy down from your soul star and expand it into your heart chakra.

THE ANTAHKARANA AND THE PILLAR OF LIGHT

The Antahkarana is the heart channel, the 13th, and most mysterious of the acupuncture meridians

The Antahkarana is the central axis of our physical bodies. It is also the central channel within the pillar of light, and the core of our "energy body" (Light Body).

The Antahkarana enters the physical body at the crown chakra, and passes through the center of the body. It exits the body at the perineum, and terminates just below the feet. At times of intense meditation it can be projected into the earth's core.

The Antahkarana is the etheric counterpart of the spinal column. But it is not inside the spinal column – it passes through the center of the body in front of the spine

Drunvalo Melchizedek refers to the Antahkarana as the "pranic tube." Prana is a subtle energy particle that helps to create life. It can be compared to an electron or photon.

Prana apparently moves in the field of universal Kundalini in a manner similar to electrons. Science may someday find that Prana is an energy particle that is quite similar to various subatomic particles, but that it exists in another phase of energy that is difficult to detect with 3D instruments.

Orgone energy is sometimes referred to as Prana, but no one is really sure. Many of the top scientists I the world have expressed theories that support the theory of some type of "ether" or a parallel phase of energy.

The blue aura seen in numerous photographs taken in Boynton Canyon may be Prana. The *Orgone Handbook*, by James Demeo has a photograph taken of an astronaut walking on the moon that shows a blue aura surrounding the astronaut. Dr. Demeo theorizes that this is Orgone. Willhelm Reich, discoverer of Orgone, died in prison while being held for contempt of court, his books were burned, the year was 1956.

Is the core of our being our heart or our mind?

One of the paradoxes is whether our true I AM awareness resides in our heads or our hearts. Shaman's, and other mystics soon discover that the body itself has an awareness, and the guts are not just along for the ride. The liver, kidneys, ovaries etc. have powers and awareness of their own.

I watched former Apollo orbiter commander, astronaut Timothy O'Leary bend a spoon with psychic powers like Uri Geller. Dr. O'Leary is a PhD. physicist .He claims that our hearts control the power that made the molecules in the spoon tem - porarily melt, and that this power is love.

As human beings we are naturally telepathic.

It is generally accepted among the schools of mystic thought that the primary reason the average person is not aware of the psychic energy they are constantly broadcasting and receiving is that their conscious mind filters out these signals. Many reasons may be given for this filtering, but the most obvious cause is that most people are trained from childhood to ignore psychic energy and concentrate on the sensory input of the physical sensory organs.

Telepathy is prayer! When we focus our thoughts on Divinity and send out thoughts in the form of prayers we are practicing telepathy and communicating with the Universal Mind of God and our soul. Students on the path who are a bit more advanced than the common Sunday school student may also work on sending telepathic messages (prayers) to angels, extraterrestrial groups, and inner-plane masters.

As you develop your psychic abilities, you will discover that your body is an antenna for various types of spiritual energies, and that at all times your body is sampling and reacting to the vibrations that surround it. Your heart will know many things before your mind gets its first clue. You will find in particular that you will be able to sense the physical presence and temperament of other humans with your body. This is known as listening with the heart.

Be aware of the fact that our bodies are energy beacons that attract various forms of nonphysical life. When a human is filled with love and joy, positive enti-ties are attracted into their spiritual circle. On the other hand, if a human becomes immersed in negative thought forms, their aura becomes a beacon that may attract negative discarnates who feed on the energy that negative emotions produce.

Chapter 6

Metaphysics: A Scientific Philosophy

Metaphysics is an ancient scientific philosophy that has been studied by all great philosophers, theologians and scientists throughout history. It has only been in recent times, however, that these teachings have separated from the mainstream establishment churches in the Western world and have begun proclaiming a more complete understanding of that which we call God.

Metaphysics itself is a clearly defined and highly respectable field of scientific philosophy that has been practiced by wise men, scientists and theologians throughout history. In fact, the study of metaphysics has been the basis for the scientific philosophies of many of history's well-known thinkers, including Plato, Aristotle, Pythagoras, Sir Isaac Newton and Professor Albert Einstein.

The deeds and beliefs of these great minds should be sufficient to demonstrate to all that metaphysical philosophy and the science of metaphysics represent valid fields of study for those who wish to understand the ultimate truths of existence. But it is particularly interesting and ironic to note that Harvard University has recently released Sir Isaac Newton's personal diary, which clearly states that he studied the Kabbalah, which he referred to as "Egyptian metaphysics."

The irony here is that, not only is Sir Isaac Newton the "father" of many important scientific theories, practices and the mathematic descriptions of quantum mechanics, he is also considered to be the founder of the school of thought known as "scientific materialism." It is this popular school of thought that is primarily responsible for promoting the theory that the universe is dead matter and that human consciousness is merely a chemical reaction in the brain. The irony here is that Master Newton obviously had a firm belief in the living nature of the universe, and if he could be with us today he would be thoroughly dismayed by the agnostic philosophy of many of today's scientists.

In rethinking the legitimacy of metaphysical thought it is also interesting to note the work of Professor Albert Einstein. While he never professed to be a metaphysician, his works indicate that he had a profound intuitive knowledge of advanced metaphysical principles. In fact, in our modern era, Professor Albert Einstein stands out as one of the greatest metaphysicians of all time, as he not only revolutionized the science of physics and mankind's view of the nature of reality, but also because he based all of his theories on "the observer."

This is because Professor Einstein was acutely aware of the fact that all things in the universe are based on the subjective experience of the individual, the "I Am" observer. Like all great minds, Albert Einstein came to the very metaphysical, very magical, very shamanic realization that nothing matters except that which is within the field of individual experience. It is as Don Juan said to Carlos Castaneda, "Each person experiences a separate reality." What this means is all that matters to the individual are those things that directly affect their awareness. The final result of this philosophy is the belief that through the application of the "Metaphysical Laws" individual humans can create any reality they choose.

One can easily imagine that the world would be a much better place if more people were ready to accept the fact that they can control their own lives through the application of Metaphysical Laws, and fortunately, it seems that people are waking up to this fact on a grand scale. Suddenly, here in America and in many other countries, a lot of people are beginning to show signs that our species is becoming evolved to the point where we are ready to grasp at the Infinite.

As for the word "metaphysics" itself, we find that this phrase originated during the time of ancient Greece. According to the Encyclopedia Britannica the literal translation of the word metaphysics is: "What comes after physics." This translation seems to miss the mark a bit, and I will suggest that we instead think of metaphysics as "what is beyond physical reality." In relation to this it should be noted that the early Aristotelians also referred to metaphysics as "the first philosophy," which is, of course, the study of God as the nature of the universe.

It is also interesting to know what the Greek roots of the word *philosophy* are: *philos* and *sophos*. *Philos* meaning love, and *sophos* meaning knowledge. The word *sophos* is derived from the name of the goddess of wisdom, Sophia. Therefore, the philosopher is a "lover of wisdom."

Today, metaphysics is recognized on the university level as a legitimate, well-defined scientific philosophy that attempts to understand the nature of the universe. Nonetheless, the parameters and meanings of "metaphysics" are widely misunderstood by just about everyone who has not had formal training in the actual science of metaphysics. To clarify our terms, I will state that at our current level of language use in our society there is a large difference between the words "metaphysical" and "metaphysics."

The word "metaphysical" can denote anything that has to do with phenomena coming in from, or associated with, the nonphysical realm, including the quantum forces of subatomic physics. Metaphysical phenomena can include many things that people in the consciousness movement may be interested in, including all psychic phenomena such as ESP, channeling (mediumship), psychic reading (fortune-telling) and out-of-body experiences such as astral projection. Many people, including those who are interested in Native American teachings or the teachings of Don Juan, may refer to the metaphysical realm as "spirit."

Metaphysics as a scientific philosophy of the application of spiritual laws of cause and effect can be said to include magic or any form of reality control, such as shamanism or advanced Native American teachings, as well as certain aspects of meditation, yoga, astrology, hands-on healing and all other things that involve "spirit" or the metaphysical God-forces that create reality.

There are two main branches of metaphysics: speculative and practical (otherwise known as philosophical and scientific, respectively). These two aspects of metaphysics are, however, in no way mutually exclusive. and while a student of metaphysical philosophy may never become deeply involved in the scientific application of metaphysics, a metaphysician who is also involved in the scientific application of metaphysical principles will always have an understanding of metaphysical philosophy. This book is primarily concerned with the practice, or scientific aspects, of metaphysics in relation to elevating the consciousness, increasing the vibrational state of the body and consciously creating reality.

To understand the science of metaphysics the student must accept the fact that there is no separation between the individual and the universe, and that the universe is a unified whole in which all seemingly individual units experience existence as aspects of the greater unity. Taking this a bit further, we find that as a consciousness entity each human being has the potential to operate as a self-realized co-creator with the Universal Mind. The implications of this are, of course, somewhat beyond the earth-bound comprehension of the materialists, the agnostics and those who do not philosophize.

A classic study of the science of metaphysics involves the understanding and use of what are commonly referred to as Metaphysical Laws or Universal Laws. I have found that I prefer to refer to the Metaphysical Laws as Universal Truth Principles, because the word "law" has been misused and maligned in our society to the point that it has developed many negative connotations.

The interpretation of the Metaphysical Laws or Universal Truth Principles, is of course open to a great deal of philosophical debate. In this discourse, however, we will not engage in much debate over these principles; instead we will move forward and explore my interpretations of the basic Universal Truth Principles as they were taught to me.

In exploring these Universal Truth Principles we must understand that they are philosophical interpretations of the workings of the Universal Mind, the I AM, and therefore **these principles define the mechanics of the universe itself**. When the student understands these principles they can use them to interpret their experiences on their life path, and, perhaps more importantly, use these principles to create realities that are truly in harmony with the source of all things and therefore more nurturing and enjoyable.

The understanding and application of these principles represents the basis for all forms of reality control in high magic, mysticism and shamanism. Perhaps the most notable difference between the modern metaphysics of soul star teachings and the practice of magic or shamanism is that we do not usually work with spirits or lesser gods, preferring to go directly to The Source: GOD.

Learned metaphysicians interpret the primary aspects of the Universal Mind as love, light and life. As simplistic and "New Agey" as this might sound, this belief system is both profound in its implications, and ancient and proven to be true by metaphysical philosophers of all eras.

To understand metaphysics is to understand the universe. The universe is life and light, created and sustained by love, and all things that we can comprehend are parts of the unified whole of the universe. There is no separation between man and nature; all are ONE. The universe is filled with life and light that continuously strives to expand, multiply and diversify. The program for universal life and the accompanying desire for self-preservation is evident in all things. Even rocks can be seen to have an existence as living beings when it is understood that "dead" matter is alive within the body of the universe.

LOVE, as a consciousness program for universal creation, manifests in nature as unity, harmony and joy. Understanding the unifying nature of love is an important aspect of metaphysical philosophy: God is love. To express love in one's heart and life is to be in harmony with the universe and the highest universal principles. When we achieve Christ Consciousness we are in complete harmony with all things and beyond duality. Love is the strength of the universe. The universal love of God sustains all light and life in the universe, and all things in the universe know the love of God through the **joy of existence.**

In the study of sacred geometry the metaphysician sees love as the "consciousness program" of the Universal Mind which unifies all things. It is as many great scientists have said: "There appears to be a unifying principle in nature that operates in an intelligent manner." The metaphysician sees this as the Universal Mind in action.

Beyond the discussion of the philosophical ideas associated with love, learned metaphysicians know that we all experience well-defined and easily recognizable energies that are known to be aspects of the threefold flame of universal love, life, and light. In the various schools these aspects of **universal life force energies** are commonly referred to as Chi, Ki, Kundalini, Prana, and Reiki. Love as an energy is also known to create an emotional/energy response which is referred to as "Ananda," or joy.

The orgasm is a well-known effect of the energies we refer to as universal love, life and light. When a human reaches sexual climax, each cell in the physical body temporarily opens up to a heightened state of receptivity to universal love, life and light that carry the very noticeable energy frequencies of the emotions we call bliss and joy (Ananda). Sexual union is often spoken of as "the first initiation" as it puts us into contact with the creative forces of life.

The existence of universal love is somewhat more difficult to prove to the uninitiated than the existence of universal light and life. While light and life are self-evident, we find that love manifests as a decidedly more transcendental quality that is difficult, if not impossible, to isolate or quantify as a "metaphysical energy" on any type of laboratory equipment that I know of. Because of this, many establishment scientists as well as agnostics and atheists deny that love is a universal quality, or that love has anything at all to do with the formation of the universe.

The denial or acceptance of universal love represents a primary departure between the philosophies of the materialists and those who believe in the existence of God. This dichotomy also represents an aspect of the most profound question that any human can ponder: Are we merely the product of chance evolution in a universe of dead matter, or are we aspects of a greater, divine being? Whatever the case, belief in either philosophy represents an act of faith.

When attempting to prove whether love exists as a universal force beyond the subjective reality of our individual minds, we must be willing to admit that at this point there is no scientifically verifiable proof. The belief in universal love is somewhat of an act of faith, because love can only be detected within the body, by the senses.

Nonetheless, every spiritual master, channeled entity or school of mysticism that has any notable lineage or reputation says that love is the force that creates and unifies all things, and that faith is the quality we need to cultivate in order to understand the truth of universal love.

Following this line of thought a little further, we find that according to the teachings of the Master Christ, love is an aspect of the Holy Spirit. To an earth-bound human the Holy Spirit represents the mystery of mysteries, the ultimate power of creation that emanates directly from the Godhead. In light of this it is also interesting to note that in the original Greek and Aramaic languages of the New Testament the phrase that is translated as Holy Spirit, could be more properly translated as "Holy Breath." The Holy Spirit breathes life into all things. The Holy Spirit is universal life force energy.

Love is the primal element of creation that works in harmony with light and life to create all the universes of the universe. Love cannot be quantified by earth-bound humans; it is a transcendental concept that must be accepted as an act of faith and experienced within the body and mind. Therefore, we are taught that the best thing we can do in relation to the Holy Spirit is to honor It and consciously encourage It to flow through us at all times.

In metaphysical philosophy it is understood that there are two primary forms of love: conditional love and universal (or unconditional) love. Conditional love is a strictly subjective experience that occurs within the mind of the individual; it is a form of attachment, desire and judgment. Therefore, in the Buddhistic sense, conditional love is very much a part of the transitory world of illusions.

Universal love is the basic quality of the primal God-force that creates all things. In its simplest definition, love is the *will* to create. It is the directive of the first thought produced by the Universal Mind: "Let there be light."

Universal light is therefore an aspect of universal love. It carries the program of love throughout the universe. In metaphysical meditations, the meditator, through an act of *will,* and under the guidance of a human teacher or master such as Christ, learns how to attune themselves to the pure love-light of the universal Creator. Universal light is also known to be the primary manifestation of all life in the universe. This includes light itself, both spiritual and physical, all matter, stars and planets.

We must also understand that the ancients equated the soul of the human with the energy of the stars. It is no accident that the Latin word for the sun is *sol.* Each one of us is an aspect of the love, light and life of the Creator of all things, the entity that the Master Christ referred to in his native language as "Abba," or Father. **The energy that creates stars is the energy that creates souls.** To activate the body of light/merkaba is to merge the physical body with the higher self, which is an aspect of the body of universal consciousness: the soul.

Universal love is the *will* to create, and then nurture (sustain) all life. Love is seen to be the most primal and important aspect of God. Love is universal life and light in action. and the universe experiences joy in the realization of its own existence.

The natural product of universal love in action is the desire for self-preservation. The desire and command to preserve life is seen as the primary truth in the universe. For humans the universal law of self-preservation manifests in four primary ways: the desire to preserve our individual lives, the desire to experience life as joy, the desire to create offspring (or to simply create), and the desire to achieve a continuation of our consciousness beyond the earth realm in the ever-expanding life systems of the universe. This process is known as ascension. Christians refer to ascension as "everlasting life," the ultimate form of self-preservation.

A common thread woven through all schools of metaphysical philosophy is the concept of "Logos." The word Logos denotes the creative power of the Universal Mind. This word comes to us from the ancient Greeks and in its most literal sense Logos means "word." The power of "the word," or language, has been recognized in all schools of philosophy and spirituality as the ultimate concept that any individual is capable of comprehending, because all things within the individual field of awareness in each person's mind are expressed as the dialogue of self-awareness, or language.

The primary reason that the metaphysician, the mystic, the magician, or the shaman needs to be aware of the all-encompassing implications of language is that it is through language that each individual interfaces with the Universal Mind; that to control language is to control reality: I speak, therefore I am.

The control of reality/experience through the understanding of the use of language is a vast subject that can only be learned in stages. At this point let it suffice to say that meditating on the reality of awareness itself is an excellent exercise. It is very empowering to realize that the "I am" within each one of us is an aspect of the greater I AM that is the universe, and that there is no part of our being which is not part of the universe, all are one!

As such, we find that a basic principle of metaphysical philosophy is that, as an inseparable aspect of the infinite universe, there is no reason why any human should be limited in any way, and that the only reason we are limited is because we limit ourselves with faulty beliefs about the nature of reality. To overcome this, students must erase many "programs" that they have accepted from social training. and they must find new ways to language the *image* of reality that they wish to attain. At this point I feel that for modern Americans the best techniques for re-imaging reality are those of the various schools of Neurolinguistic Programming.*

Mind is a concept that is inseparable from language. Mind expresses itself through language, and it must be realized that self-awareness cannot be accomplished without language.

Language is not, however, the exclusive realm of dialogue as it appears within our minds. Language includes all concepts of which a human can be aware: earth-bound, spiritual and transcendental. Therefore, language should be understood to have a very large definition that can even be said to be multidimensional.

As a demonstration of this we must realize that all forms of energy contain information, and therefore, language is energy. The structuring of the energies that comprise the universe can be expressed as a language of mathematics and geometry that is imprinted on the basic energetic force of the universe as a whole. This is the psychological structure of the Mind of God.

* Advanced Neuro Dynamics, 1833 Kalakua Ave. #908, Honolulu, Hawaii 96815

In the application of metaphysics the student needs to understand that every-thing is energy, and that through the basic energies that create our universe our minds interface with all things. For proof of this we can look at Professor Ein-stein's work and the theories of quantum physics. and as all energy contains infor-mation, we can see that energy itself is a form of language. Einstein also correctly theorized that the universe is a "unified field" of energy. Taking this a step further, metaphysical schools speak of the universe itself as the Universal Mind. This de-notes the fact that the universe itself is a self-aware entity which expresses itself as awareness in energy, form and life.

The classic teaching is that the Universal Mind expresses itself in a language that manifests as the creation of all things. In contemplating this we are reminded of the words of St. John in the New Testament: "In the beginning was the Word, and the Word was with God, and the Word was God." and does not the very word "world" come from the root – word? All that is, is language.

In application, to control the language dialogue within our consciousness is to control the way we perceive reality; for in fact, each individual conscious-ness-entity creates their own universe within their own mind. Each individual knows only what they perceive. So it must be understood that all things that are perceived exist as language within the mind; language is the vehicle of perception. The implications of this are profound. All great philosophers, scientists, seers, mystics and magicians know of this concept and work with it in their own ways. The language/perception equation is the key to all things.

The most important concept to be aware of in this discussion (or anything else, for that matter) is that everything in the known universe is based on the observa-tions of the observer (the I Am within each of us). Einstein and Don Juan were acutely aware of this. Einstein said that "Everything is relative to the position of the observer," and Don Juan said that each person experiences a " *separate reality.*" (and all observations and pictures of reality are structured in language.)

For the sake of clarity it must be understood that language is not the exclusive realm of dialogue as it appears within the human mind. Not only does language in-clude all concepts of which a human can be aware – earth-bound, spiritual and transcendental; language (apparently) also involves Universal Mind concepts that are completely beyond the realm of human perception or speculation. Therefore, language should be understood to have a very large definition that can even be said to be multidimensional.

We must also realize that all forms of energy contain information, and there-fore, language is an aspect of energy. The structuring of the energies that compose the universe are interpreted by human observers as a dialogue of mathematics, ge-ometry and harmony. When considering the higher aspects of universal creation, mathematics, geometry and harmony are seen as the foundations for the manifesta-tion of the human experience on any dimension, and that which we call mathematics, geometry and harmony are constructs created by the Universal Mind which produce the orderly formation of the love, light and life in the manifestation of All That Is.

The reality that our mind perceives appears to be built from physical objects. Upon investigation, however, we find that while it is difficult to scientifically iso- late or quantify the existence of nonphysical (or metaphysical) forces such as life force energy or universal consciousness, it can nonetheless be demonstrated that in-depth deductive and scientific analysis of physical reality reveals a great deal of evidence that seems to indicate that there is an *informing principle* or *intelligence*, evident in all natural phenomena. It is this informing principle that metaphysicians refer to as the Universal Mind.

In metaphysics the existence of the Universal Mind is taken to be a basic fact. The universe is not believed to be made of dead matter with no intelligent motiva- tion; it is instead taught that the universe is a living, self-aware entity. The unified field of energy that is the universe is love, life and light. The universe does not cre- ate matter, stars, starlight, planets and life by mere chance. It is instead a self-aware entity that consciously creates a myriad of multidimensional realities.

From the human perspective, mathematics and geometry form the basic patternings of the primal energy that creates our reality. Each atom of our body is a waveform conceived according to perfect unified principles that evidently hold true in all regions of the known universe. The Universal Mind is everywhere, cre- ating, informing and empowering all things with love, light and life.

When contemplating the reality of the Universal Mind we must realize that mind is a principle that is inseparable from language. Consciousness is impossible to achieve without dialogue: "I think therefore I am," and so forth. It is from the understanding of these concepts that the ancient Greek philosophers began using the term "Logos" (which means "word") to describe the Creator of all things. It is also interesting to note that the principle of Logos, or the creative word, was recog- nized by the apostle John: "In the beginning was the Word, and the Word was with God, and the Word was God."

It should come as no surprise that the word "God" itself has an interesting con- nection to the study of metaphysics. The word God is a derivative of the Hebrew letter Yod, which is "Y" in English. The letter Yod is symbolic of the flame, and in its written form it actually resembles a curling flame, (or dare I say a spiraling vor- tex of fire?) The flame symbolized by Yod has a great deal of significance. It is symbolic of the primal energy that creates all things, and the divine fire that illumi- nates all creation with the sacred light which carries forth the Wisdom and *Will* of the Creator of All Things.

 – Yod

The flame symbolized by the letter Yod is also symbolic of the inherently masculine nature of the primal God-force that stretches forth to impregnate the primal void of the Goddess of space. It is love, light and life. The flame is also symbolic of the lingam, and it is from the linguistic root lingam that we get the modern English word "language." Language, in its highest meaning, denotes the creative power of the Universal Mind, the Logos, or God. For in reality these three words define exactly the same thing.

The Yod, or lingam, represents the singular nature of the Godhead which enters into the universes of creation as the threefold flame of love, light and life. It is because of their direct connection to the Godhead that love, light and life are known to be absolute universal truths. It is from this awareness that metaphysicians have discovered the universal truth principle: "*light is truth*."

In application, *light is truth* tells us that The Light (or energy) that emanates directly from the Mind of God is known to be the pure essence of the ultimate truth of existence. Therefore, when humans consciously begin working with "The Light" they become illuminated with the absolute truth of the Universal Mind, which is expressed in the language of light. This pure energy from the Great Central Sun has the ability to transcend third-dimensional blockages and thereby re-imprint the student with the higher light codes of pure love that automatically cleanse and purify our bodies of energy blockages and negative mental conditions, such as the "big three:"sin, guilt and fear.

When working with light, the student must be aware that many schools of spiritual thought teach that light can also be used by entities who do not have humanity's best interest in mind. Therefore, if we desire protection from negative forces we must remember to qualify our spiritual work with invocations of the Master Jesus Christ, the avatar of the true New Age.

Qualifying energy is one of the most important parts of this work. It is therefore suggested that at the beginning of each meditation or ceremony you pray out loud and ask that only entities who serve the Creator of love and eternal life and who work for the *positive evolution of humanity* respond to your prayers. As a daily routine or at least a few times a week it is also beneficial to meditate on the reality of the being we call Jesus Christ, who was known in his time as Joshua or Eshua Ben Joseph (Joshua, son of Joseph). As an aid to this we may use pictures of Jesus, but we must realize that these pictures are like a map; they are only representations of the real thing. No one I know of is certain what Jesus looked like, although we may have a reliable guide for this in the image found on the Shroud of Turin.

The information given in **The Keys of Enoch** *serves as a bridge between the Infinite Mind of God and the minds of humanity. The information given in the* **Keys** *transcends everything the common earthling has been taught. It is the teaching for our age; it is the ultimate manual for the ascension.* The *Keys* are available from the Academy for Future Science, P.O. Box FE, Los Gatos, CA 95031

The *Book of Knowledge: The Keys of Enoch*, published and taught by **the Academy for Future Science**, is one of the most unique books in the planetary library. Dare we allow ourselves to believe that *The Keys of Enoch* is in fact exactly what it claims to be: a direct communication from the highest celestial hierarchy, delivered to this planet by the angelic orders of Metatron, Michael, Melchizedek and Enoch under the direction of the Source Creator of all things?

In the introduction to *The Keys of Enoch*, Dr. J.J. Hurtak makes the declaration that he was given the *Keys* during an experience wherein **he was taken before the Throne of God by an interdimensional light vehicle known as a Merkaba.** Dr. Hurtak does not claim to be the author of the *Keys*, instead, he states that the *Keys of Enoch* are the creation of one of the aspects of the Godhead called Metatron.

The Keys of Enoch is therefore Metatronic science, providing the disciplines to create and completely restore life systems of creation in the outer universes. *The Keys of Enoch* refers to Metatron as the visible manifestation of The Deity. Metatron is the Logos, the Creator of the Divine Word and an aspect of what most Christians, Jews and Muslims might call God.

Upon examining *The Keys of Enoch*, it becomes difficult to imagine that they are the product of Dr. Hurtak's imagination. The *Keys* are complex, scientific and detailed. They provide interesting and plausible explanations to our big questions, such as, what is the nature of God, how God creates the universe of universes, how and why human beings were created, and why, in spite of the fact that we are told that God is infinitely wise and loving, there is hate, anger, and disharmony.

Dare we allow ourselves to imagine that *The Keys of Enoch* is truly a direct communication from God? Why not? The *Keys* certainly do not tell us to do anything most of us would consider to be bad. In fact, the *Keys* encourage us to take a deeper look at the teachings of the Master Christ and the Old Testament. Dr. Hurtak informs us that *The Keys of Enoch* was brought to us at this time because our planet is indeed in a time of transformation that will take us beyond all of our current definitions of reality, and that we are in fact being retrieved by the celestial hierarchies and rescued from the distortion of existence in the outer universe.

The Keys of Enoch offers humanity a scientific and religious understanding of this process. It can be understood in its simplest terms as working with the feminine aspect of divinity, the Holy Spirit (Shekinah), in establishing a pillar of spiritual light around the body that forms a bridge between the body and the Christ Overself (Atman Soul).

The Keys of Enoch is based upon the science of understanding language as the structure of reality. Everything we can know exists as language. Consciousness is language. Without the dialogue of self-reflection, consciousness cannot exist. Language/consciousness originates from the Universal Logos, Metatron, as the Master I AM threshold commands. *In the beginning was the Word, and the Word was with God, and the Word was God.*

The Infinite Mind of God expresses itself with pure energy emissions, the living language of light. This language of light exists on all levels of creation from sub-atomic to cosmic, organizing the Holy Spirit, Shekinah, into the harmonic structure of the universe. Language creates the patterns that create reality.

The language of living light functions as the bridge between our limited third-dimensional minds and universal God-consciousness. The highest level of mystical knowledge is the understanding of language as the structure of reality. To have total control of the use of language in speech and thought is to have total control of reality (see the teachings of Don Juan). Language is energy, and all energy is a form of language (see Jose Argüelles' *The Mayan Factor*). Language creates and connects all facets of the universal energy matrix. The study of sacred geometry is one aspect of understanding the universal language of light.

In the three-dimensional reality of planet earth, the language that comes closest to expressing the true language of light is Hebrew. Key 305:22 tells us that "The sacred language is thoughts of God." Key 215:63 tells us, In essence the flame scriptures (of Hebrew) were composed out of "living geometries of God's Word, extended to connect with the vibratory resonance grids of the earth."

DIVINE ATTUNEMENT and DIVINE PROTECTION

KODOISH, KODOISH, KODOISH, ADONAI SEBAYOTH

Key 305 of *The Keys of Enoch* tells us that the mantra "Kodoish, Kodoish, Kodoish, Adonai Sebayoth" (Holy, Holy, Holy, Lord God of Hosts) is the measure and cycle of all states of matter/radiation, and that it creates resonance between all levels of creation and the primary Source Creator. Those of you who are familiar with the New Testament's Book of Revelation and the vision of St. John will recognize Holy, Holy, Holy, Lord God of Hosts as the mantra chanted by the four entities surrounding the throne of God.

The Keys of Enoch states that Kodoish, Kodoish, Kodoish, Adonai Sebayoth ties all rhythms of the body together with the spiritual rhythms of the Christ Overself. When we chant this mantra, our Christ Overself bodies are quickened into direct work with the physical body. It is suggested this mantra be incorporated into our daily meditation practices, as it is known to be the most important key to divine attunement. (Key 305:7, 26, 28, 36.) Kodoish, Kodoish, Kodoish, Adonai Sebayoth should be used to discern the spiritual from the negative forces. In fact, this salutation is so strong that negative forces cannot remain for any length of time in the presence of its vibration.

The Keys of Enoch were delivered to humanity through Dr. Hurtak as a result of his contact with a Merkaba piloted by Angelic Beings.

The *Keys of Enoch* states that on one level, the entire universe is a Merkaba. and the grand spiral of space and time is sustained by The Merkaba, which contains a multitude of smaller Merkabas that all work in harmony to provide interdimensional coupling between the consciousness controls that emanate from the Throne of God and all other dimensional realities.

The energy patterns that we will study in the sacred geometry sections are produced by the Divine Template of energy encodings that are carried by The Merkaba through the various dimensional thresholds into our reality. The Merkaba is the "crystal within the crystal." It is responsible for transmitting the threshold commands from the Most High that produce the protein matrix codings of human DNA, which in turn create our physical bodies. We were put in this dimensional reality through the action of the Merkaba and we will be retrieved through the action of the Merkaba.

Individual Merkabas within the greater Merkaba of time and space can become "high-energy vehicles" of the highest extraterrestrial interstellar and interdimensional intelligences, such as angels. The appearance or the manifestation of the Merkaba should never be confused with the comparatively low-level existence of the common physical UFO. The Merkaba is unquestionably identified with the Powers and the *Will* of the Most High Lord God Creator of the Universe of Universes and the Elohim Lords of Light that serve the Most High.

Key 205:33 tells us that three "Whole Light Beings" (Elohim) work with each individualized Merkaba and that these beings will belong to the orders of Michael, Metatron, or Melchizedek.

To access the energies of the Ascension, we must invoke the Merkaba with ceremony. Key 115:40 tells us that when ten faithful beings are gathered together they can create a Merkaba which will bring with it two spiritual guides that will take the group into the next level of intelligence. These guides, will be Elohim of the orders of Michael, Metatron, or Melchizedek. Presumably, the third entity of the Merkaba remains in the higher dimensions. (See Key 301.)

I have lead a number of ceremonies where it seemed that our group was definitely receiving energy from a source like a Merkaba. I feel that this is the highest expression of the medicine wheel ceremony, *the medicine wheel of light.*

The Academy for Future Science website – http://www.affs.org

Chapter 7

Vortex Mysterium

As I slept, an ET crept into my dream.... Hello, I come in the name of the One. I would like to do some things with you. May I? This is a test.... Strange energies began flowing through my body, causing me to shake. As my conscious mind merged with my dreaming mind, I became happily amazed by the reality of the situation. I was having a dream that was unlike any other I had experienced. I was sharing a dream with a strange alien entity!

As my consciousness shifted from the dreaming world to the here and now, I began losing contact with the alien. I felt I was failing the test so I sent the ET a thought: More, give it to me, I can take it! I think my outburst startled the entity a little, and soon the dream disappeared.

I awakened, still shaking, feeling very connected to the energy of the dream. My mind was racing. It was incredible! I had just had an astounding paranormal experience. AN ALIEN HAD COME INTO MY DREAM!

I was amazed! Science fiction had become reality; I had been contacted. There was no doubt in my mind that my dream was real. For whatever reason some sort of alien intelligence had come into my dream and done something to me that had made my body shake as if it were being supercharged with life force energy.

I had not experienced any pain during this dream, but upon awakening, and ceasing to shake, I found that my body felt like it wanted to lie still and integrate the energy. I was exhilarated! I had been zapped by an ET while sleeping. Soon I found myself wide awake and I was very excited. I knew that the entity who had come into my dream was standing beside my van at that very moment.

My mind raced. I had no doubt that I was in telepathic contact with an ET. **I knew** that a strange creature was just outside my van, **I knew it**. I was so sure of this that I did not even get up to look out. Can you imagine that? My little earthling mind was blown! I did not even get up to see the ET! **I knew it was just outside the window**; I did not have to look. **I knew it**. I simply lay still in wonder and amazement, sensing the energy in my body.

After a short period of time I began to come more into the here and now, and thought about taking a look; but then, if I looked, I might be compelled to go outside the van and face the alien in the flesh. This frightened me a little, as I had heard that aliens sometimes are pretty rough on humans, so I just lay still.

After a few moments I felt strongly compelled to look, but I still refused to do so. Soon the energy shifted again and, suddenly, something gave a single knock on the rear door of the van, just inches from my head. Immediately I knew that this knock was a signal that I could trust my feelings; an ET was present.

At that point I knew that the ET was going back towards the vortex and if I wanted to see it this was my last chance. I stayed in bed. I never looked out but **I knew it was there.** I did not need to look. (But if I had, I think I would have seen a typical short, bug-eyed, big-headed wierdie.)

All this occurred while my girlfriend, Karen, slept next to me. I allowed more than a year to pass before I told her what had happened. This event was so extraordinary, perplexing, magical and personal that I decided to keep it to myself. Yes, Sedona is a strange place, and science fiction does sometimes become reality.

This event took place in 1989, at the Airport Vortex. Since the time of this encounter I have had plenty of time to think about my experience, and I am glad that I did not attempt to make contact. I now realize that this event could have ended up with me on the cover of the *National Enquirer,* with the headline:

SEDONA MAN MADE PREGNANT BY SPACE ALIEN!

(Or perhaps something worse.)

A SPECIAL NOTE FOR THE YEAR 2000 EDITION

As many philosophers have said, knowledge can be a great burden. For a number of years I have actively sought knowledge about the mysteries of existence and the place of humanity in the universe, and I now find myself almost overburdened with knowledge, much of which is far too esoteric to be included in this book. I also think it is true that certain levels of understanding cannot be conveyed in a book, and true wisdom or insight into the nature of reality is something that one *arrives* at. So let me please attempt to tell you, in as few words as possible, what I believe to be true in relation to UFOs and the nature of reality.

We are definitely not the only sentient beings in the universe, and it is certain that we share this planet with other forms of sentient life, who may, or may not, be from another world. Those who argue otherwise are simply not aware of the facts— or are very much aware of them and are, for whatever reason, lying. In regard to this I will add my observation that most of the people who write for major publications or bring us the news are not qualified to write on subjects related to the paranormal, so if one bases their belief on what they have read or seen in major media they will be badly uninformed and misguided.

The existence of these beings challenges the traditional Western view of the world and the basic premises of Christianity and its predecessor, the Hebrew faith. While it is certainly true that these religions speak of a God and angels that are presumably from a place beyond our planet (thus making them "ETs"), the enormous amount of information that has been gathered about the non-human beings we are encountering indicates that many do not fit neatly into the category of either angel or God.

There is evidence to suggest that humanity is involved in an ongoing battle between the forces that support our life and the forces most would term evil, and that this is a mind game of tremendous proportion freaky enough to cause hordes of people to jump out of that proverbial window if only they knew a portion of the truth. As it is said, ignorance is bliss, so I salute those who find it easy to write off people who believe in UFOs as fools. Dream on.

There is a tremendous amount of evidence to suggest that humanity is being manipulated by what can best be described as alien mind control, that this has been going on for some time, and that a great deal of what is taught in our religions, philosophies and channeling is tainted. In regard to this I suggest seeing the 1999 film *Matrix*, and allow yourself to believe that there is an element of truth to this movie, which *is largely based on information given by Carlos Castaneda at his historic six-day intensive which he gave at UCLA in 1996* (I was there...).

I am hopeful, however, that God as an absolute force in the universe does exist. That God has humanity's best interests in mind and that there is Divine Grace and the healing power of the Master Christ. For if these things do not exist, humanity is in very deep trouble. It does appear that the forces who are apparently attempting to destroy humanity are being held at bay by other forces that are benevolent toward humanity, so we can therefore take heart that all is not lost. Perhaps it is as *The Keys of Enoch* states: our planet is in a realm very far removed from the Godhead, and because of "time lag," changes ordered at the top appear to take quite awhile to trickle down. I sincerely hope that the power of love exists as a force that overcomes the forces of negative evolution.

Some of the strange creatures who manipulate humanity may not actually be from another planet, but as most of the mythology surrounding them claims that they are from "somewhere else," perhaps we can allow ourselves to believe that they are. Since flight between the stars may be more difficult than we imagine, perhaps we could allow ourselves to imagine that these entities might be from another planet in our own solar system and *not* from the stars. Ancient texts and mythologies indicate that what is now the asteroid belt may well have been a planet destroyed by a cataclysm triggered by forces and civilizations that led to the destruction of the ecosystem of the now-barren planet Mars. Dare we allow ourselves to imagine that these same forces are currently behind the scenes helping us to destroy our lush island of life in a cosmos of vacuum?

There have been various reports of paranormal activity in the Bear Wallow Canyon/Schnebly Hill area. Usually we simply refer to this area as Schnebly Hill. Most of it can be seen from Uptown Sedona, and West Sedona. This canyon is a wondrous work of art, containing thousands of intricately sculpted rocks and inspiring vistas which give the viewer no doubt that Schnebly Hill is an enchanted place.

The most beautiful Sedona alien-contact story I have heard took place below Schnebly Hill, just beyond the mouth of the canyon. I feel fortunate that my friend shared this story with me, as it is of a personal nature.

She had been attracted to Sedona for some time and was finally able to arrange a visit. My friend is close to her mother and asked her to come along. When they got to Sedona her mother began to feel ill with a minor heart problem that she had suffered with for some time. They spent their first night in Sedona at the Cedars Resort, which is just below Schnebly Hill. During the night my friend had a dream that she was holding her favorite crystal in her hands over her chest and that there was a UFO outside the window. It was beaming some type of Light energy through the window and into the crystal which, in turn, reflected the Light into her mother's chest. As in my own experience with aliens, my friend awoke to find that this was really happening! She immediately began shaking, which caused the connection to be broken and the beam of Light to disappear. She and her mother were astonished! Adding to their wonder, they noticed that there was indeed a bright object in the air a mile or more away, up the canyon.

The next day her mother felt much better, and it is my understanding that her heart condition has improved. Can you imagine something like this happening to you? I have heard stories of other paranormal healings in Sedona, and I believe that there are entities here who occasionally perform healings on humans. One can only imagine what type of entities these might be.

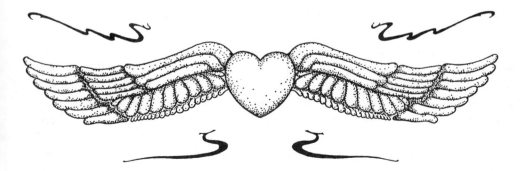

Among UFO researchers it is commonly believed that the United States Government operates underground bases in cooperation with extraterrestrials. Because of this, and the fact that our area is a known center of UFO activity, it is natural for us to suspect that the black helicopters commonly seen flying over Sedona are part of a covert operation. What we find however, upon investigating the situation, is that for the most part there is a rather mundane explanation for the presence of these helicopters, and that the most substantial evidence of covert operations in our area is to be found not in the air, but upon the ground.

For years, psychics have identified the Secret Mountain area, which is just north of both Boynton and Long Canyons, as a location of some type of interdimensional portal that is used by extraterrestrial craft. Various psychics have even gone so far as to say that both positive and negative extraterrestrial factions have bases in the Secret Mountain area. and as there have been numerous sightings of UFOs in the Dry Creek area, just to the south of Secret Mountain, it is commonly believed that the psychics are correct. Because of this, it does seem particularly odd that we see so many military helicopters coming into the Sedona area from the direction of Secret Mountain.

When we first started seeing the black helicopters and speculating as to what their mission might be, most people did not realize that there was a National Guard base just north of Sedona. All we knew was that several military helicopters flew through the area each week, and they often seemed to be either heading toward, or away from Secret. After awhile, however, some of us got out our maps and discovered that there was a base in our area. This discovery, of course, did nothing to lessen the mystery of the helicopters; in fact, it seemed to add to it. An army base is just a few miles north of Secret Mountain; how interesting.

As speculations and rumors about the mission of the helicopters became increasingly more exotic, however, my truth detectors began to tell me that some of the things I was hearing were the product of someone's overactive imagination. Finally, I decided to take the proverbial **bull** by the horns and pay the base a visit to see if I could gather any information.

Upon arriving at the base I found that I was truly impressed by its somber atmosphere. There was also not much to see, as most of the buildings on the base are small, earth-sheltered bunkers that are used to store munitions. After entering the main office I encountered a group of officers in the hall. It was perhaps as strange for them to see me there as it was for me to find myself there. With my long hair, beard and purple sweater, I looked the total antithesis of an Army man. They did not seem too disturbed by my presence however, and after talking to them for awhile, they suggested that I have a private conversation with one of the colonels who was there with us.

After we stepped around the corner to his office, the colonel and I had a pleas-ant conversation in which I learned that the Navajo Weapons Depot consists of lit-tle more than 450 earth-filled bunkers that contain various types of conventional munitions; that on the average, maybe one helicopter lands at the base each week, and that if they do land in the area, they usually do so at the civilian airports in ei-ther Sedona or Flagstaff. I also learned that most of the helicopters we are seeing are not black, but dark green, (which can look black from a distance). The colonel also informed me that the main base for the helicopters is the National Guard base in Phoenix, near Papago Park. (It is public knowledge that the Papago base is an underground installation.)

I had told the colonel that I was a local writer and that I was doing a story about the helicopters. I explained that there had been a lot of sightings and some reports of people being chased out of canyons in Sedona by either helicopters or armed men wearing black jumpsuits which appear to have military insignias such as red triangles affixed to the arms and the chest.

I also told the colonel that a rumor was circulating around Sedona that there was some sort of covert operation in the mountains just north of Sedona and that I had come up to the base to see if I could learn anything. (I never mentioned UFO's.) The colonel may have been somewhat cautious in what he had to say to me but it did not seem that he was lying when he told me that the Navajo Weapons Depot is not a helicopter base, and that he knew nothing about any sort of military activity in our area being conducted by an apparently covert force.

The colonel suggested that if the stories were true, and that if there were indeed some type of military activity in the canyons, it might be a civilian paramilitary force. I agreed with him that this could be true, but the use of helicopters seemed beyond the financial capabilities of America's weekend militia. He did not have an answer for that but he did seem sincere about his lack of knowledge on the subject of secret bases, and I believe he had no knowledge of covert activity in the Sedona area.

The colonel did ask if anyone had called the Sheriff after being accosted at gunpoint and I had to tell him I had no idea. **We both agreed that any time one is threatened by gun-brandishing men they should notify the local authorities that they have been assaulted.**

After giving the colonel a phony name I bid him farewell and headed back to Sedona in my car. Yes, I thought to myself, the colonel had certainly seemed sin-cere, yet I knew my visit had neither proved nor disproved anything.

A few weeks later I contacted the Public Information Officer at the Arizona National Guard base in Phoenix, and found that most of the helicopters we see in the Sedona area are on normal training missions (which are usually on weekends) or are being used to bring supplies to remote areas in northern Arizona that are pe-riodically isolated by winter storms. Most of these helicopters are Vietnam-era, Huey UH1s, or dual engine Blackhawks. Occasionally, one of the ultra-modern

Apache helicopters that are stationed at the National Guard base at Marana in southern Arizona may also come through Sedona's skies.

Die-hard conspiracy theorists will of course never accept mundane explanations for the military helicopters that pass over Sedona, and I think that this is perhaps a good thing; we should always question the intentions of the government and the military. It is the American Way. This is how we keep our freedom. Yet, we must ask ourselves why, if the helicopters are involved in a covert mission, do they make no attempt to avoid being seen flying in from the area of their alleged base? Why do they frequently refuel at the Sedona airport, and why, after refueling, do their crews have lunch at the airport restaurant?

FOLLOW UP FOR THE YEAR 2000 EDITION

Sometime after my book *Sedona UFO Connection* was published a friend of mine related the following story to me. I believe that this story is true and that it confirms the existence of the underground base.

My friend, a young woman in her 30s had a relationship with a man who, while hiking in Secret Canyon, was accosted at gunpoint by a soldier wearing a United Nations insignia. A few days later, my friend and several of her friends, including the man who had been accosted in Secret Canyon were dining at the Hideaway restaurant when a group of soldiers walked in wearing camouflage uniforms! The young man who had been accosted recognized one of them as the person who had threatened him with a gun, but instead of calling the police to report the crime, he just left the restaurant in fear.

The fact that these soldiers boldly walked into a popular restaurant in full uniform seems to indicate that whatever the purpose of the underground base, it must not be too big a secret. Those who are interested in conspiracy theories will of course take note of the fact that these soldiers wore United Nations insignia and spoke to one another in a foreign language.

CLOSE ENCOUNTERS IN THE DRY CREEK AREA

One of the most fascinating UFO sightings to come out of Sedona thus far was witnessed by a friend of mine in the summer of 1992. This story may be seen to provide us with a valuable clue as to what is going on in Sedona and what is happening in regard to our government's alleged involvement with extraterrestrials.

My friend and another man were in the Dry Creek area hoping to see a UFO. (Secret Canyon is also in the Dry Creek area, as are Boynton, Long and Fay Canyons.) Suddenly, in broad daylight, a flying disk appeared over Capitol Butte heading north toward Secret Mountain. What makes this sighting particularly amazing is that the flying disk was being accompanied by four fighter jets in formation!

My friend and his partner were astonished! It was unbelievable! Imagine their surprise when the four jets broke away from the flying disk and the disk shot straight up into the air and disappeared!

This story, however, does not disappear into thin air. The gentlemen who witnessed this event were newcomers to Sedona. The one I know had been in town for about six months at the time of the sighting. The other gentleman had been in town about a month. We will call him Wolfdancer as that is similar to the name he used. Mr. Wolfdancer was a big man who had served in Vietnam. He was an outlaw who had become metaphysical. He had come into town with a bunch of crystals and was trying to make a living selling them at a table at the New Age Center. That is where he met my friend.

Wolfdancer had just spent several months around Mt. Shasta, California, where he had spent a great deal of time hanging around with a video camera in hopes of filming UFOs. He had indeed found a few to film. In fact, my friend said that Wolfdancer not only had footage of numerous craft flying around Mt. Shasta, he also had footage of what appeared to be portals opening up near the summit of the mountain and UFOs flying into them! Apparently Wolfdancer had a knack for being in the right place at the right time.

A few days after Wolfdancer and my friend sighted the flying disk and the fighter jets, two gentlemen visited Wolfdancer's camp. They appeared to be some type of military men dressed in civilian clothes. They told Wolfdancer that they knew what he was doing and he had better stop. A few days later Wolfdancer disappeared and has never been heard from again.

My friend feels that Wolfdancer has been abducted. It is my understanding that Wolfdancer had indicated to various people that he was going to stay in Sedona for some time. He had made various connections with people that suggested he was quite intent on staying here. My friend is certain Wolfdancer had no plans to leave town. He also knew that Wolfdancer had no money to do so even if he wanted to, as he was down to less than twenty dollars cash, which he had borrowed from my friend a day or two before he disappeared.

I have no idea if anyone has spoken to the authorities about Wolfdancer's disappearance. My friend hasn't, and I haven't. I never met the man and had only seen him around town. How can I report someone missing when I don't know him? It is important to note that Wolfdancer lived in his van. When he disappeared, his van disappeared. He lived outside of society and vanished without a trace. Perhaps you would like to go out to Secret Canyon and look for him.

If you do decide to go out to Secret Canyon and play James Bond, you should, by all means, make sure your life insurance is paid and your will is in order. You should also remember to tell someone where you are going and when you plan on returning. Then, when you disappear, we will have another confirmation of our theories. Be a good citizen - don't let your abduction go unnoticed!

Many UFO researchers have presented material that suggests the government of the United States is in contact with extraterrestrials and that our government may have agreements with some groups that allow them to build underground bases in return for antigravity and other types of advanced technology.

The flying disk accompanied by fighter jets may well be an example of alien technology being adapted by earthlings. As for the manner in which the flying disk disappeared, we may theorize that there are some type of portals in, around, or above Sedona that can be used to jump between the space/time location of Sedona and points unknown, but presumably in other star systems.

The Keys of Enoch tells us that all gravitational bodies are connected by **stralim** (lines of gravitational force) and that interstellar/interdimensional craft operated by the hierarchies can travel almost instantly between points that are con-nected by the stralim. We may theorize that the vortices of Sedona have something to do with stralim that connect earth to other star systems. This theory is in har-mony with information given by many channels. As an example of this, I refer the reader to *The Sedona Guide Book,* published by Light Technology. Various chan-nels in *The Sedona Guide Book* claim that there are several points around Sedona that act as portals for various groups of extraterrestrials that come to earth from distant stars.

Following this theory a bit further, we might allow ourselves to believe that one of the reasons that the military may be present in Sedona is that they may be at-tempting to control some of these portals.

PLACES TO SEE UFOS

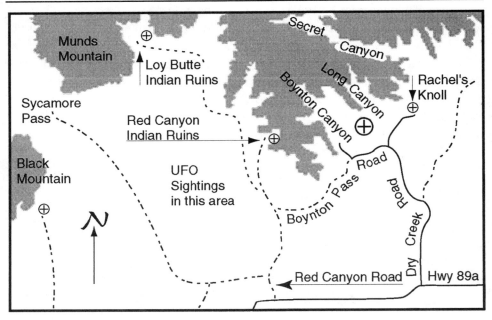

In the original *Sedona Power Spot, Vortex, and Medicine Wheel Guide* I wrote: *"Circles of stone such as this are truly one of the mysteries of Sedona. Most locals know that to build a wheel such as this is "against Forest Service rules." This leads us to the conclusion that the rocks on the medicine wheel must move into place by themselves. As further evidence of this, Forest Service officials have noted that in some cases wheels that have been disassembled by Forest Service workers have re-appeared overnight."* This was meant as a joke, but it certainly was true that a number of wheels did get taken apart and put back together rather quickly.

This particular wheel was about an hour's walk up Boynton Canyon. Since this picture was taken, this wheel was permanently disassembled by the Forest Service. This wheel annoyed the local Indians and was a violation of the Federal wilderness area laws (no man-made structures). I was sorry to see it go, as it was a good destination and a good place to enjoy the energies of the canyon.

This letter was sent to several Forest Service employees during the formation of the new forest plan, which now prohibits camping around Sedona, and may lead to further restrictions.

I know that you are all intelligent, educated and well-meaning, and will probably have a degree of agreement with some of my criticism. I also understand, that you must take into consideration various bureaucratic and academic concepts that I may know nothing of....

I am the author of the most widely-read book on the subject of the vortex phenomenon in Sedona, and the founder and leader of the Sedona Vortex Society. Older editions of my "vortex book" request that my readers write me a note saying that they support open access to public lands (meaning of course: all areas in the Sedona area). I have several boxes of letters and can produce them on request. Because of this I should definitely be seen as a leader in the community, and my opinions should be taken into account.

I am a native of Yavapai County and was born in Prescott in 1957. I grew up in Scottsdale. Since 1988, I have resided either in Cottonwood or Sedona. During that time I have attempted to keep track of Forest Service policy. I am also very familiar with the land itself, as I have spent a respectable amount of time enjoying it.

I attended the first meeting that the Forest Service held in regard to the new plan, and while I do remember signing a piece of paper saying I would be notified of further meetings, I was not. Partially because of this I did not manage to attend any of the other meetings, except for the last one. At the final meeting on the Forest Service plan I spoke at length to Peter Pilles and Marrietta Davenport. I also had the chance to ask Ken Anderson a question. While I understood that it would be impossible to answer my question, as it was actually a series of questions, I believe I made a point that was well understood by most of the people in the room except for Ken.

My questions began with this question: **"How do you feel about the Magna Carta and the Right of Passage?"** Mr. Anderson claimed to not know what I was talking about, but several people in the room did remember their high school history, and King Henry the VIII.

What we need to understand in this matter of the proposed Forest Service plan, is that along with the other rights which American citizens supposedly have, King Henry's peers believed that humans have the right to occupy land that is held by the government. and while our constitution does not give us this right (unlike British subjects) everything we are taught about government as children implies that we do have the right to use the forest, even to the point of using it as a residence.

*The current proposals for the Forest Service plan not only scoff at what our forebearers felt to be an absolute right, it also favors developers, and creates "**pay-per-view tourism**" that will effectively shut out many people who will not be* *able to afford to stay in hotels or expensive time-share developments. Indeed, a segment of our society is to be thrown off the land to make way for development that we could quite correctly refer to as pay-per-view. The new rules will also ad-versely affect many individuals who are capable of paying, but who would rather get right out on the land.*

One of my primary complaints in regard to how the Forest Service has handled Sedona is that in all the areas in question there has apparently been given very little consideration as to how to actually improve the public's enjoyment of the red rock areas (see below). This is more of a question of philosophy, rather than budget, and I feel that these questions need to be addressed.

From the advent of Sedona being discovered by the New Age, the philosophy of the Forest Service, under former District Ranger Bob Giles, has appeared to be one that **purposefully maintained conditions that lead to the "trashing" of all the areas in question**. This subsequent loss of topsoil and plantlife, as well as a lit-eral trashing of certain roadside camps, has lead to a situation in which the Forest Service can now say it is their duty to close the areas due to misuse.

While individual employees of the Forest Service would deny that it has ever been the intention of the Forest Service to purposefully create conditions that have lead to today's proposed closures, I will suggest that once individuals become part of a government bureaucracy they may well become blind to the fact that their good intentions are being overshadowed by a very real and demonstrable bureau-cratic desire for control and enforcement.

One of the stated goals of the Forest Service is to enhance the experience of in-dividuals when they visit the National Forest. Unfortunately, like every Govern-ment bureaucracy, the Forest Service's true mission of service to the public has become rather distorted. In this case, service has focused on control and enforce-ment, instead of true enhancement.

The proposed Forest Plan brings us into some very interesting philosophical territory, as the current crisis has obviously been manufactured, with the predetermined end result of **"necessary new policies" that limit the enjoyment of the traditional users of the Forest** – *those who camp* – **in favor of upscale tourism and more development.**

As for the Dry Creek area specifically, isn't it ironic that the campers are get-ting chased off, and that the developers are (perhaps) going to be able to develop the entire 300 acre strip between the Tree Farm and the Cockscomb. **I am certain that even as a Forest Service employee you can appreciate that this particular land trade idea stinks.**

As for Schnebly Hill Road, now that the plan is complete, and I have time to put this all in perspective, it is evident that the Forest Service never wanted to en-courage camping in the area because it is seen as a future route for a paved road.... So we are to lose a great camping area to the cars....

To accomplish the aforementioned goals, the Forest Service has maintained a posture of "not having the funds to provide any services (except enforcement) in this area." I challenge any Forest Service employee to convince me that the district could not have used the yearly salary of one employee, such as a GS 5 (who now start at $20,495 a year) to both construct a toilet facility up there and put in a couple of dumpsters. My point here is that it is not really an issue of money, it **is an issue of philosophy**, and the philosophy of the Forest Service in general has not been one of true service to the people who enjoy the forest for recreation.

As final note on this subject I will mention the Back O' Beyond area. As camping is to be banned there, this will fit in well with the plans of the folks who are currently developing the area; after all, it is important for them to get the riff-raff out in order to maintain and enhance the property value in that area....

As a Forest Service employee, you are aware the Coconino National Forest has allowed extensive clear-cut logging on the mountains directly adjacent to the Sedona area. When I mention this to a Forest Service employee such as yourself I will be told that logging as a detriment to the forest, and tourist use as a detriment to the forest, should not be equated. As a citizen I find this to be classic double-think.

and then there is the issue of cattle grazing which the Forest Service has allowed in Sedona for a number of years. We all know that the cattle grazing has been *the* major offender to the topsoil, yet we find the Forest Service loath to admit it, instead choosing to blame it on their favorite culprits, the public.

History shows that government bureaucracy invariably strives to make citizens into criminals. In regard to this it should be noted that the various regulations will obviously be scoffed at by the citizens who enjoy the forest. This will result in charging many individuals with crimes such as trespassing.

I want the forest service to create facilities that improve and enhance the public's enjoyment of the forest, not restrict it. Build campgrounds.

Richard Dannelley

Chapter 8

The Medicine Wheel Of Light

Black Elk, the great Sioux Indian warrior and teacher, had a powerful vision in which he saw that all groups of people will someday come together within "The Sacred Hoop of the Nations," the medicine wheel.

THE MEDICINE WHEEL AND
GEOMANTIC EARTH HEALING CEREMONIES

I find it quite interesting that so many people have become attracted to Native American teachings and the medicine wheel in the past few years. I see this as a result of two things: first, many Americans of European descent have strong past-life connections to Native American culture; secondly, we know intuitively that ceremonies that are similar to the medicine wheel open up interdimensional portals that allow the Christ Consciousness energies to enter the planetary grid.

As for the concept of Americans of European descent having past lives as Native Americans, this seems to be in harmony with the law of karma and the prophecies of various Native American seers from the 1800s to our current days. Thus, it is plain to see that at this time in our history a large part of our national karma has to do with reconciling the beauty and the pain of the native peoples. It is therefore very healthy for those of us who are of European descent to participate in ceremonies such as the traditional medicine wheel, the sweat lodge, and the pipe, etc., but we must avoid getting trapped in the past and remember to keep moving forward into *new interpretations of that which is so ancient.*

Most Americans of European descent who study Native American teachings follow the medicine wheel teachings of the plains tribes that are similar to those which were taught by Sun Bear. These teachings are beautiful and powerful, but it must be understood that for the most part they reflect their originating tribe's interpretations of the universe, which in many ways were valid only for those people in the days when they lived. This is why I neither follow nor attempt to teach the old tradition: those days are gone.

The medicine wheel ceremony is the application of the same technology that creates the Merkaba. In the final phase of ascension, the medicine wheel becomes the Merkaba of ascension, a jeweled vehicle of redemption from the lower worlds.

Every person who reads this book knows that this planet and its occupants are currently going through a very critical phase of accelerated evolution. A vision has been given to many of us, telling us that it is time to bond our energies together in prayer and ceremony to create an energy field that will stabilize our planet and bring peace to the hearts of men.

It is time for those of us who can hear the call to establish an energy network (web) of medicine wheels around the globe. By bonding our energies together in ceremony we will create a powerful energy field which will affect the group consciousness of humanity.

The rules of ceremony vary among various tribes and traditions, so it seems that no matter how one performs their ceremony there is always someone else who thinks it should be done a different way, and that the directions have dif-ferent colors and meanings. So instead of giving a detailed, dogmatic descrip-tion of how to do a ceremony, let us just touch on a few of the basics.

The act of entering the wheel separates us from our daily routine and ordinary reality. When we enter the wheel we are in a magical space: It is the temple of God and Goddess. Look inside yourself and find the truth of your heart, and use your prayers to give that truth back to the universe.

At the beginning of each ceremony a prayer should always be directed to the Great Spirit, the four directions, the father (the sun), and the mother (the earth). Remembering that there are many names for these entities, I suggest you use the names you feel most comfortable with.

The tradition which I am familiar with begins with a prayer giving thanks and then asking for guidance, protection and blessings, first from the Great Spirit, and then the four directions, beginning with the east then moving around the wheel in a clockwise direction, to the south, the west and then the north.

Each tribe has different names for these entities, so you should use whatever names you feel most comfortable with. After prayers have been given to the direc-tions, the father (the sun), and the mother (the earth) are honored.

I am also convinced that the land has spirits, and that these Devas and Kachinas feel honored to be invited to sit in the four directions and help hold the energy of the wheel, and that this helps bring good fortune in all affairs. These enti-ties also respond to offerings, and corn seems to work well, although I have met a couple of Kachinas who also like *Goldwasser.*

After the opening prayers it is often a good idea to play drums, chant, or sing, in order for the group energy to become unified and harmonious. I usually get my groups to chant OM, Aloha and other words of power.

While people are "up" and the energy is high, it is time to conduct a guided light meditation which invokes the light of Christ to fill the participants' hearts and all others across the planet. After the initial invocation of light, specific people, places, etc. can be focused upon to receive love and healing.

There are many interpretations as to what quality the directions have, so I sug-gest that you focus primarily on higher concepts such as simply communing with God, Goddess, the angels, the archetypes, the stars, and universal love, leaving the Native American teachings of animal spirits, tobacco offerings, etc., to those who belong to that culture. (Sage smells nice but it is not a require-ment for ceremony as the energy fields you will be generating will clear the space quite well.)

The word "medicine" as it is used in the term medicine wheel, refers to the healing power of spirit and love.

The circle and cross design is a symbol of universal love. It can also be used as a type of antenna to bring positive energies into the earth and our homes. Mandalas from India and Tibet are based on the circle and cross design, and simply hanging some of these mandalas and yantras in your living space can have a positive effect on your environment.

One of the most important factors in building a medicine wheel is the energy you put in to it. A wheel that is worked with on a regular basis is going to have a stronger field than one that is not. If you have a yard or a garden, you might find that building a wheel seems to enhance the positive energy around your home.

It is important to remember that if a wheel is built in an area where anyone can have access to it, it can be misused. It is therefore important to disassemble any wheels that are built in a public place after the ceremony is complete.

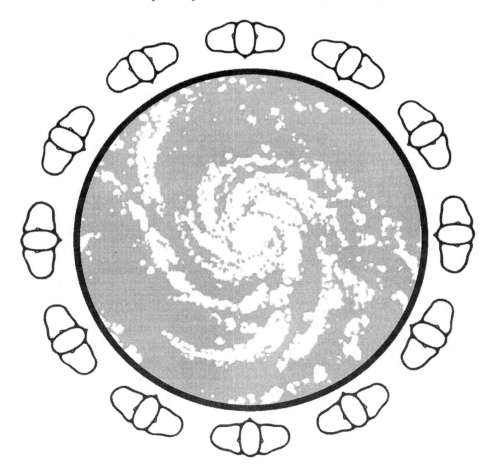

Selecting a proper site is important, but it is not always necessary to find a place that is already a place of power. Human beings are able to draw power into a place, thus creating a power spot. You can build a medicine wheel in your back-yard, and if it is used regularly for prayer, meditation and ceremony, it will become a power spot, a wheel within a wheel in the web of life.

When you start looking for a place to build a wheel, ask yourself and your friends if they know about any places nearby in the countryside that are known as a power spots. Follow your heart, and remember that people are drawn to power spots naturally. Choose a place, and bless it with prayers.

Any time you start a wheel, it is important to bless the sacred ground with prayers. Be sure to banish undesirable energy from the area by invoking the power of the Great Spirit and the presence of Christ.

Native Americans recommend burning sage as an incense to drive out 'bad' spirits. If available, liberal amounts of sage smoke can be applied to all participants in the ceremony, and to the sacred space itself. But be assured, cleansing invoca-tions and the power of Intention are just as powerful and effective.

⊕   ⊕   ⊕

Driving a stake in the ground to mark the center of the sacred ground is the first ritual of the wheel, symbolizing the descent of spirit into matter and marking the center of the sacred ground.

After that, tie a string or a rope to the center stake, and scribe a circle on the earth, thus establishing the boundary of the sacred ground.

Aligning your wheel with a magnetic compass is the easiest way to find the four directions. We know that true north (geographically) is not magnetic north. But if your wheel is aligned with the magnetic field of the earth you can be sure that you are resonating with the magnetic flux lines in that area.

Ancient geomancers probably marked the cardinal points by observing the shadow cast by the center pole as the sun rose and set on the days of the equinox. The north and south points can then be determined by dividing the circle between the east and west points, or by using the north star.

It is not always necessary to build a medicine wheel with physical objects such as stones, and sometimes, particularly in city situations, building a stone circle can be very impractical and even undesirable. (You never know who may come along and desecrate the temple.) Powerful energy fields can be raised just by gathering a group of people together in a circle with ceremonial intent. Permanent architecture is unnecessary. Crystals, or other special rocks and objects, can be carried to cere-monies, and then returned home with their keepers.

⊕   ⊕   ⊕

Our galaxy, the stars, our solar system, our planet and the human body are all aspects of the spiraling energies of the universal Merkaba. The Mirror-twin spirals of DNA are one of the best examples of the universal Merkaba/vortex energy patterning. It is also interesting to note that the chemical bonds of DNA are composed of the same geometrical forms that are found in the planetary grid.

When I wrote my first book, *Sedona Power Spot, Vortex and Medicine Wheel Guide,* I spent many hours musing over the concept of spiraling energy. At that point I was still fairly new to this field and I did not have as much information as I do today. I had been told that it was safe to work only with spiraling energy that moved in a clockwise direction, and that counterclockwise energy fields were "negative," "dangerous," and "used by black magicians." Since that time, and with the help of various teachers, including Drunvalo Melchizedek, I have come to the realization that what I had been taught about the "dangers" of counterclockwise energy fields and the superiority of clockwise energy fields was for the most part superstitious rubbish.

The universe is in balance. The study of universal Merkaba/vortex phenomena shows us that the mirror-twin energy fields sustain one another. Neither the right nor the left is "good" or "evil," as these concepts are entirely relative to the position of the observer. Instead, these spirals of universal life force energy should be seen as nothing more than energy that is flowing through an alpha-omega cycle of complementary polarity and expansion/contraction.

What Drunvalo Melchizedek helped me understand is that it is important to work with both spirals in order that we remain in balance. Clockwise energy fields draw energy into the center point of the vortex. Clockwise energy brings space into order. Counterclockwise fields expand energy out from their center, and can be used to dissolve structures.

Kryon, a popular channeled entity, tells us that the vortices in Sedona are part of one large counterclockwise vortex that spirals through the valley. *This might help to explain why we find Sedona energizing, as counterclockwise vortices release energy.* It also might help explain the politics in Sedona and why the New Age community here remains so fragmented and disorganized: counterclockwise energy can dissolve structure.

It is interesting to note that if one were to observe our planet from above the north pole in space, it would appear to be moving counterclockwise. This direction of rotation might be essential for the maintenance and expansion of life.

Within the precise geometries of the planetary grid there is a more subtle, ir-regular and organic network of energy lines that connect a myriad of individual power spots together. Many of these places are areas of concentrated life: forests, jungles, and cities. Natural geological features, such as rivers, valleys, mountains, mineral deposits and faults also create natural gathering places and channels for currents of life force to circulate within the grids.

In regard to our work it is important to note that lines of energy within the grid can be worked with, created, or made stronger through prayer, meditation, and cer-emony. One of the main purposes of this book is to inspire groups and individuals in as many places as possible to begin consciously projecting love and Christ Con-sciousness thought-energy into the grid and the center of the earth with pillars of light.

When we begin working with the universal life force energies and the grid ,we move into a realm that requires not so much analysis as it does instinct and emo-tion. Working with universal life force energy is an intuitive process that is refined through practice and guidance. The study of the geometrics of the planetary grid is important because it demonstrates that there is indeed an underlying intelligence in nature; but ultimately we need to go beyond descriptions and analysis and get into the energies themselves.

SEEKING GUIDANCE FROM THE MASTERS

The spoken word and intention are two of the most powerful tools that we can use to make our ceremonies powerful and effective. Throughout the world, mystic traditions rely on prayer and intention to "qualify" the energy of ceremonies, to in-voke guides and to direct energy. The ability of prayer to qualify energy is one of the most important concepts to be aware of. To qualify energy is to ask for what is wanted (or not wanted). Qualifying energy with prayer will program the Universal Mind to send you what you ask for.

As an example, if you want to work with Christ energy, and therefore be pro-tected from all things negative and undesirable, ask out loud that the Master Christ be with you and that all other guides and masters that are drawn to you serve the Master Christ, and work for "positive human evolution, and ever-expanding life."

As another example, let us imagine that you want to work with universal life force energies for the healing of the planet, but you do not have much experience doing so. In such a case it is appropriate to ask for guidance:

I ask that the Universal Mind guide me in accessing these energies,
I ask for guidance from the Master Christ,
I offer myself in service to the healing of planet Earth.

Merkaba fields, pillars of light and other types of energy fields, such as grid connections, can easily be brought into manifestation through an act of intention, *will*, and visualization. Beginners can start activating their abilities by using the following invocation: "I activate the circuitry within my mind and my light body that controls my ability to work with these forces."

We can create individual or group pillars of light using the powers of intention, *will* and visualization. In group ceremony the leader can ask in prayer that a pillar of light be placed over the group and that each individual in the group receive guidance in accessing these energies and creating the pillar of light. Sound, such as the Aloha chant, should be used to tune up the pillar of light.

After the pillar of light has been invoked, the power of *will* can be used to make this energy expand and grow. As the universal life force energies in the energy field builds they automatically cleanse and purify the individuals in the ceremony, particularly if invited to do so. After the participants are cleared, the energy can then be expanded to cleanse and purify the home or ceremonial area, and then further expanded in stages to purify and empower the local community and countryside. It is also highly recommended that the pillar of light be used to send universal life force energies into the center of the earth.

Some of you who read these words are natural leaders and teachers, so I encourage you to put the concepts in this book to use and organize a group. What I have found over the past few years is that more and more people are becoming open to the possibilities that exist, regardless of the fact they may not have experience or training in working with these energies. It seems quite natural for people to want to come together in prayer and ceremony for the healing of the earth.

Remember that prayer and intention control these energies: When you send love energy into the grid or connect your wheel to the grid, you do not have to know what the mechanics are or which route the energy should take. Instead, make a prayer asking for the desired result and know that it is being done automatically.

The group merkaba/medicine wheel techniques given in this book should be considered to be phase one of what is possible. I am certain that these ceremonies can have a powerful effect on both the participants and the planet. Because of this I encourage you to put the information about the group merkaba/medicine wheel to use, by organizing a planetary healing group in your area.

Chapter 9

Planetary Grid

Some of the concepts and words used in this section may be somewhat complex, but if you have the desire to understand the mysteries of creation, I suggest that you read all of this material. If you do not understand some of the terms used, please refer to a dictionary. The letters UVG stand for unified vector geometry. The UVG is the basis of the planetary grid, as proposed by professors William Becker and Bethe Hagens. The word polyhedron means many angles or faces. The Platonic Solids (tetrahedron, octahedron, cube, icosahedron and dodecahedron) are all polyhedrons.

The most important thing brought to our attention through the study of the planetary grid is that this information demonstrates that all things are part of a grand universal plan that needs to be looked at seriously as a guide for structuring our decisions on managing our world. The number of connections and correspondences between systems such as geometry, biology, astronomy, etc., that are revealed by this study are immense, as all things are truly interrelated. We can only hope that the people who currently steer our course as a society (the politicians and bankers) begin to wake up to the fact that we metaphysical people have access to information that is essential to the continuation of our species.

In presenting this material, I owe a debt of gratitude to Professors William Becker and Bethe Hagens and to Governor's State University of Illinois for allowing their research to be shared with the public so freely.

One of the many interesting things that should be noted in our discussion of planetary grid research is that the ancients apparently used a system for understanding the nature of the earth that is very similar to the UVG system we are currently studying. This amazing revelation comes to us as a result of the research that was originally conducted by Professors Becker and Hagens.

Modern planetary grid research is being carried on by many groups, individuals, and governments. In America the best-known researchers are Professors William Becker and Bethe Hagens, Chris Bird (author of *The Secret Life of Plants),* and Bruce Cathie (of New Zealand). The research of Becker, Hagens and Bird was catalyzed by an article that appeared in the official publication of the Russian Academy of Sciences titled, "Is the Earth a Large Crystal?"

Upon reading the article, Becker and Hagens noticed that the Russian grid had the basic geometry of a geodesic dome. After consulting *Synergetics II* by Buckminster Fuller (a well-known engineering genius and the inventor of the geodesic dome), Becker and Hagens realized that connecting the vertices of the icosahedron and dodecahedron in the Russian grid resulting in what Mr. Fuller called a rhombic triacontahedron. This form is apparently one of the most important and primal energy patterns in our universe, and is the basic energy pattern for all spheres in our universe, including our planet.

The rhombic triacontahedron is the highest frequency regular polyhedron, as it is composed of 120 identical right triangles. These triangles are the result of 15 great circles, each of which divides the sphere into two equal halves, like the equator divides the earth. During his studies of the sphere, Mr. Fuller experimented with balloons and found that when they are inflated to near their limits and then examined closely with the proper optical equipment, their membranes will automatically organize themselves into the great-circle patterns of the rhombic triacontahedron. This indicates that the theory of universal energy patterning is more than a theory. It is a fact of nature.

Professors Becker and Hagens took the liberty of adopting a new name for the rhombic triacontahedron, calling it the Unified Vector Geometry, or UVG. All of the maps in this chapter are based on this form.

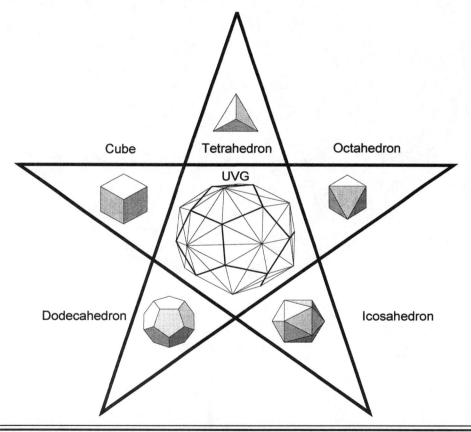

The UVG is the synthesis of the five Platonic Solids. An interesting confir-mation of the profound universal importance of the Unified Vector Geometrics is that science has discovered that the simplest of biological life forms, the virus, is enclosed in a membrane that duplicates the Unified Vector Geometrics! (As above, so below....)

The Secondary Great Circle Tracks of the UVG Create "the Web"

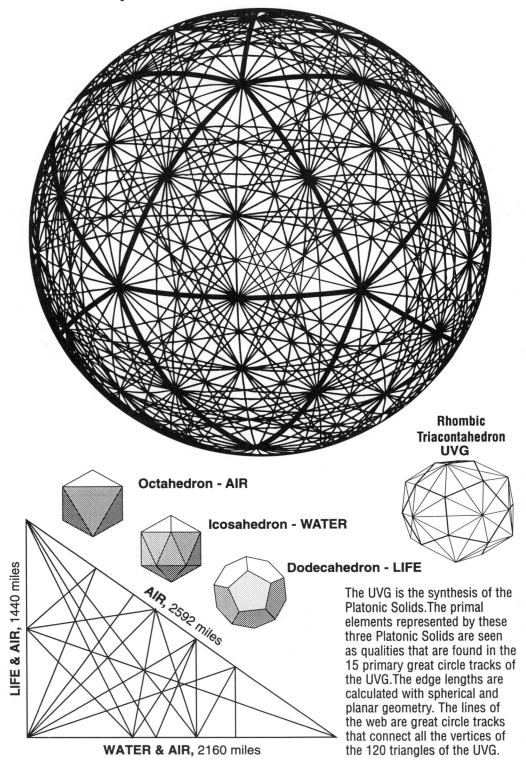

Octahedron - AIR

Icosahedron - WATER

Dodecahedron - LIFE

Rhombic Triacontahedron UVG

LIFE & AIR, 1440 miles

AIR, 2592 miles

WATER & AIR, 2160 miles

The UVG is the synthesis of the Platonic Solids. The primal elements represented by these three Platonic Solids are seen as qualities that are found in the 15 primary great circle tracks of the UVG. The edge lengths are calculated with spherical and planar geometry. The lines of the web are great circle tracks that connect all the vertices of the 120 triangles of the UVG.

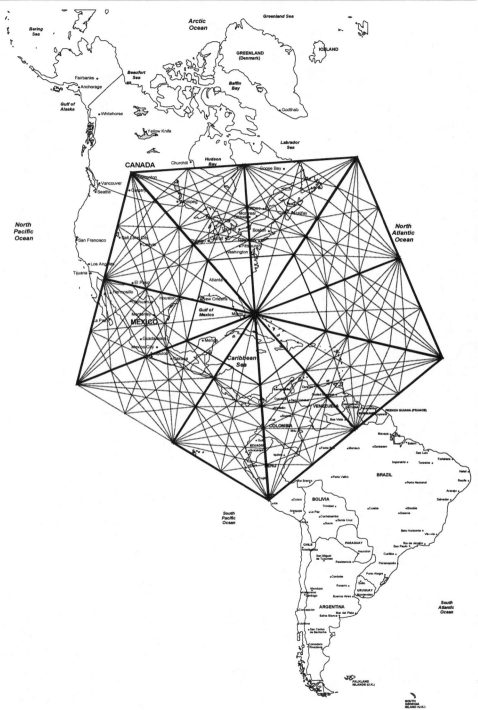

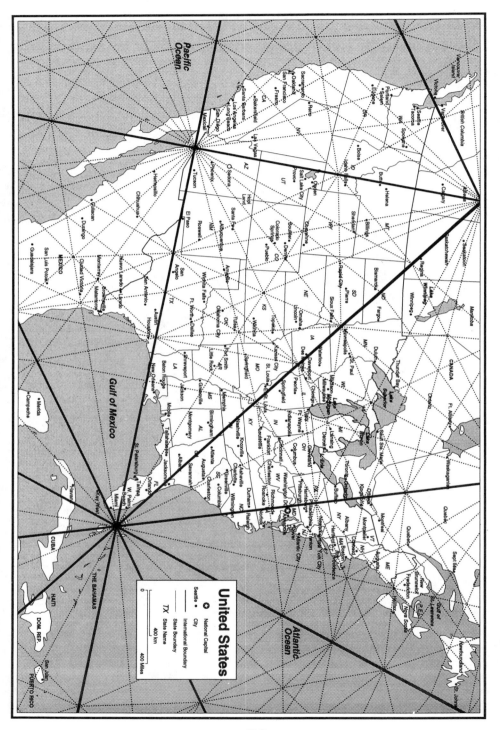

United States

⊕ Seattle National Capital
• City
International Boundary
State Boundary
TX State Name

0 400 km
0 400 Miles

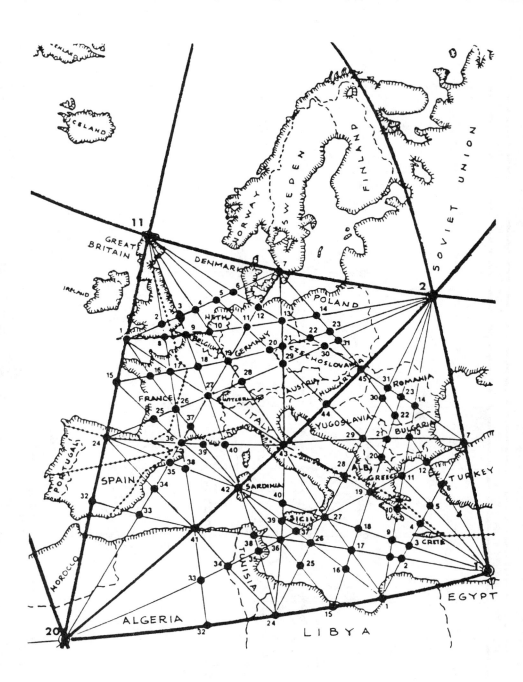

Map of Europe by Bethe Hagens and William Becker

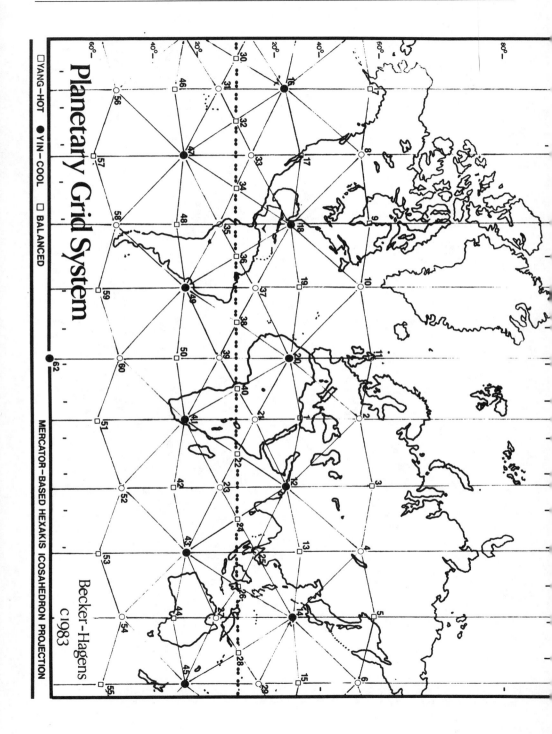

Planetary Grid System

□ YANG-HOT   ● YIN-COOL   □ BALANCED

MERCATOR-BASED HEXAKIS ICOSAHEDRON PROJECTION

Becker-Hagens
c1983

The descriptions of these points are taken from an essay by William Becker and Bethe Hagens entitled The Rings of Gaia, which appeared in The Power of Place, and from a magazine article by Becker and Hagens entitled The Planetary Grid: A New Synthesis which originally appeared in the Journal of SITU, and was later reprinted in David Hatcher Childress' Anti Gravity and the World Grid. I have expanded on some of the references, particularly in regard to Points 1 and 17. I will once again thank Professor Hagens for allowing me to use this material and acknowledge Christopher Bird for his original research and profound insight into the nature of reality.

1. 31.72N 31.20E: On the Egyptian continental shelf on the Mediterranean Sea, at approxi mately the mid-point between the two outlets of the Nile at Masabb Rashid and Masabb Dumyat. The Great Pyramid at Giza is located about 70 miles south and five miles east of this point.

This point appears to be a logical orientation point for a variety of reasons, including the fact that nodes naturally occur in the UVG at 31.72N. This point is also about 40 miles east of the site of the Lib rary of Alexandria, which in ancient times was the central point for the mapping systems discussed earlier in thi s section. It is interesting to note that the ancient maps were oriented very closely to this point, as it provides exce llent positioning for the other points around the globe.

The north-south meridian that goes through point 1 has been recognized since ancient times as the meridian that passes through the largest area of dry land. Point 1 is also precisely 2160 miles from the e quator; 2160 miles is also the diameter of the Moon and the length of the long side of a UVG grid triangle. Another interesting thing about point 1 is that it is approximately in the center of all our planet's landmasses. While this may seem interesting enough in itself, we can also theorize that approximately 240 million years ago, before the continents drifted apart, this area was also in the center of the primordial continent. This is apparently why *The Keys of Enoch* refers to the Great Pyramid as the White Throne in the Center of the World.

Archaeological points of interest located near Point 1 include the library of Alexandr ia, the Great Pyramid at Giza, King Herod's fortified palace, the Dome of The Rock, the Temple of Solomon at Jerusa lem, and Heliopolis. It is interesting to note that this area was one of the foca! points of western culture for t housands of years, and that many of the great teachers and philosophers of the past studied or lived in this area.

2. 52.62N 31.20E: Near Kiev, one of the most beloved cities of the Ukraine, this area is one of t he most notable centers of commerce, farming and mining in eastern Europe.

3. 58.62N 67.20E: Near Tobolsk in Russia.

4. 52.62N 103.20E: Near Lake Baikal, which is thought to be the oldest, deepest and largest lake on our planet. This lake accounts for approximately one fifth of this planet's fresh water resource.

5. 58.28N 139.20E: In the highlands along the coast of the Sea of Okhotsk.

6. 52.62N 175.20E: A notable United States military base exists near here at the island of At tu in the Aleutians. This area flourishes with marine life.

7. 58.28N 148.80W: Edge of continental shelf in Alaska. The line connecting this area to Point 6 coincides with a unique volcanic zone, that is roughly parallel to the Bering Straits. The massive Prudhoe Bay oil deposits are north of this point, on its northern line.

8. 52.62N 112.80W Buffalo Lake, Alberta. This is the first major intersection north of Sedon a and Point 17. This is the area of Canada's most prolific oil and gas reserves as well as its most prolific wheat-f arming area. This area is noted for its approximately 5,000-year-old medicine wheel, near Majorville.

9. 58.28N 76.80E: Just east of port Harrison on Hudson Bay.

10. 52.62N 40.80W: Gibbs Fracture Zone. Along with points 19, 37, 38, 39, 50, and 60 the lands be tween these points roughly MAP out the mid-Atlantic fracture zone. This one of the hot spots on the ocean fl oor where molten material from the inner earth is exuded. Some of the most unique forms of marine life live in areas such as this.

11. 58.28N 4.80W: Loch More, on the west coast of Scotland. powerful psychedelic mushrooms gr ow in this area. The secondary Great Circle lines that pass through this area have a direct connection to Poin t 1 as well as many other notable sites in Europe.

12. 26.57N 76.20E: Bordering the Indus River Valley, this is the area where the Hindu civiliza tion began.

13. 31.72N 103.20E: A major center of the Chinese civilization for at least 3000 years. Just north of this point, on a Great Circle track that connects this point with Point 4, are the Chinese pyramids of Xien, *which are almost exactly on the opposite side of the earth from Sedona* . This Great Circle also passes through Washington D.C. and the Bermuda Triangle. For more information on these pyramids see Bruce Cathie's *Bridge to Infinity.*

14. 26.57N 139.20E: Near Japan, in the Pacific Ocean at the intersection of the Kydshu Palau R idge, the west Mariana Ridge and the Iwo Jima Ridge.

15. 31.72N 175.20E: At the intersection of the Hess plateau, the Hawaiian Ridge and the Empe ror Seamounts.

16. 26.57N 148.80W: Northeast of Hawaii, midway between the Murray and the Molakai fracture zo nes.

17. 31.72N 112.80W: Near Sonointa, Mexico, south of Ajo, Arizona and the Organ Pipe National M onument. This point is approximately 250 miles southwest of Sedona. The Organ Pipe area has long been r egarded as a place of mystery similar to Sedona. As a word of warning I will mention that this area, and th e National Monument in particular, are considered dangerous areas because of the large amount of drugs an d illegal immigration coming across the border. So if you go there, camp only in regular campgrounds. This is still the wild west, and many locals carry guns for insurance. The last time Professor Hagens was down there she notic ed that there is a large installation of about 50 dish antennas in this area. This may indicate that the gover nment utilizes this area because it has desirable electromagnetic qualities.

I find this to be a very interesting site, not only because it the major grid intersection closest to Sedona, but also because its northern Great Circle track passes close to Prescott, Arizona, where one of the mo st notable local variations in the earth's geomagnetic field occurs. This line also passes through the Great Salt La ke in Utah, which *The Keys of Enoch* names as a contact area for the Brotherhood of Light. There is a significant junction of se condary Great Circle tracks in the Salt Lake near Ogden. This Great Circle track is also of particu lar interest because it connects with Point 12 (the Indus river valley where the Hindu civilization began) and Point 8, in Canada, which has near it an approximately 5000 year-old medicine wheel-type structure that is sometimes r eferred to as the American Stonehenge. Point 17 is also on the same latitude as Point 18 in the Bermuda Triang le, Point #1, and Point #12 (see previous paragraph).

18. 26.57N 76.80W: The Bermuda Triangle, at the edge of the continental shelf near Great Abac o Island. This north-south Great Circle track passes through Washington D.C. and the area of the pyramid s in China (see Point #13). Point 18 has direct connections to Points 8 + 35.

19. 31.72N 40.80W: Atlantis Fracture Zone.

20. 26.57N 4.80W: In El Eglab, a highland area at the edge of the Sahara Desert sand dunes.

21. 10.81N 31.20E: Sudan highlands.

22. 0N 49.2E: Somali abyssal plain.

23. 10.81S 67.20E: Vema Trench in the Indian Ocean, at the intersection of the Mascarene Ridge, the Carlsburg Ridge and the Maldive Ridge into the mid-Atlantic Ridge.

24. 0 85.2E: Ceylon abyssal plain.

25. 10.81N 103.20E: Kompong Som, a natural bay on the southern coast of Cambodia southwest of Phnom Penh. This site is near Angkor Wat, which is an ancient megalithic city that was abandoned in much the same manner as the cities of the ancient Mayans. This north-south Great Circle track passes through Thailand, Laos, Vietnam and

Washington D.C.

26. 0 121.20E: At the midpoint between Teluk and Tomini, a bay in northern Sulawesi.

27. 10.81S 139.2E: Midpoint of the mouth of the Gulf of Carpentaria.

28. 0 157.20E: Center of the Solomon Plateau.

29. 10.81N 175.20E: Midpoint of abyssal plain between Marshall Islands, mid-Pacific mountains and the Magel-lan Plateau.

30. 0 166.80W: Nova Canton Trough.

31. 10.81N 112.80W: Society Islands.

32. 0 130.80W: Galapagos Fracture Zone.

33. 10.81S 76.80W: End of the Clipperton Fracture Zone.

34. 0N 94.80W: Junction of the Cocos Ridge and the Carnegie Ridge just west of the Galapagos Is lands.

35. 10.81S 76.90W: Lake Punrrun in the Peruvian coastal highlands, the headlands of the Amazo n River. This point is near the Nazca Plains and an enormous pyramid complex which was described in the Ap ril 30, 1990, *U.S. News and World Report.* This area is close to Machu Picchu and major centers of cocaine production.

36. 0 58.80W: State of Amazonas.

37. 10.81N 40.80W: Vema Fracture Zone.

38. 0 22.80W: Romanche Fracture Zone.

39. 10.81S 4.80W: Edge of mid-Atlantic Ridge in Angola Basin, just southeast of Ascension frac ture zone.

40. 0 13.20W: Gabon Highlands at intersection of three national borders.

41. 26.57S 31.20E: L'uyenego on the Utsutu River, Swaziland. Just north of this point is Great Zi mbabwe a mas-sive ancient structure that is a focal point for Native African mysticism, sometimes refe rred to as Africa's Stonehenge. Near this point is also found what may be the world's oldest iron mine, the Ngwenya m ine. The north-south Great Circle track is the same one that passes through Point 1.

42. 31.72S 67.20E: Intersection of mid-Atlantic Ridge with the southwest Indian Ridge.

43. 26.57S 103.20E: Tip of Wallabi Plateau.

44. 31.72S 139.20E: In Australia, in a lowland just east of St. Mary's peak, which is the highe st point in the area. Near Spencer Gulf. Geophysists have recorded enormous geoelectric currents in the earth near her e in excess of a million amps!

45. 26.57S 175.20E: At the edge of the Hebrides Trench, just southwest of the Fiji Islands.

46. 36.72S 148.80W: Somewhere out in the south Pacific....

47. 26.57S 112.80W: Eastern Island Fracture Zone.

48. 31.72S 76.80W: The Nazca Plate.

49. 26.57S 40.80W: Deep ocean at edge of continental shelf.

50. 31.72S 4.80W: Walvis Ridge.

51. 58.28S 31.20E: Enderby Abyssal Plain.

52. 52.62S 67.20E: Kerguelen Plateau.

53. 58.28S 103.20E: Ocean floor midway between Kerguelen abyssal plain and the Wilkes abyssal p lain.

54. 52.62S 139.20E: Kangaroo Fracture Zone.

55. 58.28S 175.2E: Edge of Scott Fracture Zone.

56. 52.62S 148.80W: Unintsev Fracture Zone.

57. 58.28S 112.80W: Eltanin Fracture Zone.

58. 52.62S 76.80W: South America at its tip.

59. 58.28S 40.80W: South Sandwich Fracture Zone.

60. 52.62S 4.80W: Bovet Fracture Zone.

61. North Pole.   62. South Pole.

$\mathcal{P}$*anoramic* $\mathcal{P}$*oint*

Panoramic Point is a small hill in West Sedona that has an amazing 360° view of the Sedona skyline. From the top of this small hill that is almost hidden in the southern skyline we can see just about every one of Sedona's major geolog - ical features. Panoramic Point is just above Red Rock Crossing, and it seems that Cathedral Rock is close enough to touch, or perhaps glide down to.

The trails in this area are neither maintained or marked, so it will take a certain amount of trail sense to find one's way to the top. The trail is fairly easy to find, and most of it is quite wide, so you should have no problem following it.

Park at the end of **El Camino Road** and either go through the gate there or follow one of the trails that heads along the fence toward the south. There is a walk-through in the fence a short distance south of the road. **This is Forest Service land, so it is OK to go through the fence.** Just be sure to park off the road.

The first part of the trail goes through an area that is heavily eroded by cattle grazing and off-road vehicles. This part of the trail is the most vague, but after you have traveled south for a few hundred feet you should be able to find a trail leading off to the right. Almost immediately it will turn into a dirt road wide enough to be used by off-road vehicles. It takes about a half hour to make it to the to the top.

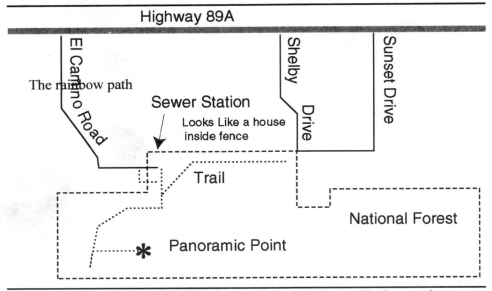

To the south we can see Bell Rock and Cathedral Rock. To the north we can see Boynton Canyon, Secret Mountain and the back of Secret Canyon.

$\mathcal{A}$*loha*